ALL OF US

A CELEBRATION OF BIPOC VOICES

---

twelve short plays by
Diana Burbano, Velina Hasu Houston, Leviticus Jelks III, Michelle Tyrene Johnson, Ramiz Monsef, Matthew Paul Olmos, Lina Patel, christopher oscar peña, Randy Reinholz, Alvaro Saar Rios, Hope Villanueva and Elizabeth Wong

curated by Jonathan Dorf

www.youthplays.com
info@youthplays.com
424-703-5315

The Day the Music Came Back © 2021 Alvaro Saar Rios; ***Linda*** © 2021 Diana Burbano; ***Phantom*** © 2021 Leviticus Jelks III; ***Anatomy*** © 2021 Hope Villanueva; ***The Mask on the Bench*** © 2021 Ramiz Monsef; ***Dream*** © 2021 Velina Hasu Houston; ***re'open our eyes*** © Matthew Paul Olmos; ***The Randomness of Bees*** © 2021 Lina Patel; ***A New Story from Rabbit and Frog*** © 2021 Randy Reinholz; ***Metalhead Thread*** © 2021 Elizabeth Wong; ***sunset on seb and hiro.*** © 2021 christopher oscar peña; ***Like A Knife*** © 2020 Michelle Tyrene Johnson. All rights reserved.
ISBN 978-1-63932-024-0.

Caution: These plays are fully protected under the copyright laws of the United States of America, Canada, the British Commonwealth and all other countries of the copyright union and are subject to royalty for all performances including but not limited to professional, amateur, charity and classroom whether admission is charged or presented free of charge.

Reservation of Rights: These plays are the property of the authors and all rights for their use are strictly reserved and must be licensed by the authors' representative, YouthPLAYS. This prohibition of unauthorized professional and amateur stage presentations extends also to motion pictures, recitation, lecturing, public reading, radio broadcasting, television, video and the rights of adaptation or translation into non-English languages.

Performance Licensing and Royalty Payments: Amateur and stock performance rights are administered exclusively by YouthPLAYS. No amateur, stock or educational theatre groups or individuals may perform these plays without securing authorization and royalty arrangements in advance from YouthPLAYS. Required royalty fees for performing these plays are available online at www.YouthPLAYS.com. Royalty fees are subject to change without notice. Required royalties must be paid each time these plays are performed and may not be transferred to any other performance entity. All licensing requests and inquiries should be addressed to YouthPLAYS.

Author Credit: All groups or individuals receiving permission to produce these plays must give the authors credit in any and all advertisements and publicity relating to the production of these plays. The authors' billing must appear directly below the title on a separate line with no other accompanying written matter. The name of the authors must be at least 50% as large as the title of the plays. No person or entity may receive larger or more prominent credit than that which is given to the authors and the name of the authors may not be abbreviated or otherwise altered from the form in which it appears in these plays.

Publisher Attribution: All programs, advertisements, flyers or other printed material must include the following notice:

Produced by special arrangement with YouthPLAYS (www.youthplays.com).

Prohibition of Unauthorized Copying: Any unauthorized copying of this book or excerpts from this book, whether by photocopying, scanning, video recording or any other means, is strictly prohibited by law. This book may only be copied by licensed productions with the purchase of a photocopy license, or with explicit permission from YouthPLAYS.

Trade Marks, Public Figures & Musical Works: These plays may contain references to brand names or public figures. All references are intended only as parody or other legal means of expression. These plays may also contain suggestions for the performance of a musical work (either in part or in whole). YouthPLAYS has not obtained performing rights of these works unless explicitly noted. The direction of such works is only a playwright's suggestion, and the play producer should obtain such permissions on their own. The website for the U.S. copyright office is *http://www.copyright.gov.*

COPYRIGHT RULES TO REMEMBER

1. To produce this play, you must receive prior written permission from YouthPLAYS and pay the required royalty.

2. You must pay a royalty each time the play is performed in the presence of audience members outside of the cast and crew. Royalties are due whether or not admission is charged, whether or not the play is presented for profit, for charity or for educational purposes, or whether or not anyone associated with the production is being paid.

3. No changes, including cuts or additions, are permitted to the script without written prior permission from YouthPLAYS.

4. Do not copy this book or any part of it without written permission from YouthPLAYS.

5. Credit to the author and YouthPLAYS is required on all programs and other promotional items associated with this play's performance.

When you pay royalties, you are recognizing the hard work that went into creating the play and making a statement that a play is something of value. We think this is important, and we hope that everyone will do the right thing, thus allowing playwrights to generate income and continue to create wonderful new works for the stage.

Plays are owned by the playwrights who wrote them. Violating a playwright's copyright is a very serious matter and violates both United States and international copyright law. Infringement is punishable by actual damages and attorneys' fees, statutory damages of up to $150,000 per incident, and even possible criminal sanctions. **Infringement is theft. Don't do it.**

Have a question about copyright? Please contact us by email at info@youthplays.com or by phone at 424-703-5315. When in doubt, please ask.

THE PLAYS

The Day the Music Came Back by Alvaro Saar Rios 5

Linda by Diana Burbano (in English and en español) 20

Phantom by Leviticus Jelks III 41

Anatomy by Hope Villanueva 55

The Mask on the Bench by Ramiz Monsef 71

Dream by Velina Hasu Houston 86

re'open our eyes by Matthew Paul Olmos 101

The Randomness of Bees by Lina Patel 118

A New Story from Rabbit and Frog by Randy Reinholz 135

Metalhead Thread by Elizabeth Wong 153

sunset on seb and hiro. by christopher oscar peña 168

Like A Knife by Michelle Tyrene Johnson 183

ABOUT THE COLLECTION

These plays may be performed individually or grouped in any combination to create a show of the desired length and performed as ***All of Us: A Celebration of BIPOC Voices***. To do every play in the collection requires 7+ performers. If each role is played by a different actor, there are opportunities for over 40 performers. Many roles are gender-flexible.

Plays may occasionally include [bracketed] dialogue which may be substituted for the original dialogue as needed.

THE DAY THE MUSIC CAME BACK

by Alvaro Saar Rios

CAST OF CHARACTERS

A.M.F.M., human, teenager.

BASS, human, teenager (character name sounds like "base").

DISCO, human, teenager.

TREBLE, human, teenager.

G MINOR, human, teenager.

SETTING

Somewhere in the United States. At least a hundred years in the future.

PRODUCTION NOTES

When possible, this play should be performed by an extremely diverse cast.

The moment where the characters hear music for the first time, the song should be unrecognizable to most of the audience.

ACKNOWLEDGMENTS

This play was commissioned by Beacon Academy.

It premiered at Beacon Academy's Spring One-Act Festival in Evanston, IL in Spring 2019, directed by Ava Dieden. The cast was as follows:

A.M.F.M..Kalman Slater
BASS...Eleanor Plunkett
DISCO..Aine Murtagh

TREBLE..Madie Morton
G MINOR..Anneke Stracks

Original Music Composition by Kalman Slater.

(Somewhere in the United States. At least a hundred years in the future.)

(We are in an empty space.)

(As the play begins, we see A.M.F.M. telling a story. G MINOR, DISCO and TREBLE listen.)

A.M.F.M.: Went to go visit her again at the hospital. My grandmother. Went last night to see her. My parents didn't know. Snuck out and went straight there. She looked tired. Maybe that's why she finally told me.

She said her favorite singer was a woman who looked just like her mother. Long hair. Brown eyes. And her smile was one that made you forget all the troubles in your life.

My grandmother can't remember what her last name was. She said everyone only knew her by her first name anyway. Selena.

(Everyone in the space repeats "Selena" as if it is a chant.)

The first time she heard Selena's mmmmmmmmm...her mmmmmusic was when she was five. Heard it on a player in her house. She said in those days, everyone had at least one. Said the government even let you turn the player on. But only on Sundays, though. You couldn't listen to it any other day. On the last day, the day before the beginning of the Days of Silence, that was the first time my grandmother heard Selena's voice. Even though it's been over a hundred years, she says she still hears her singing.

(Bang! A noise is heard offstage. Beat as everyone remains still.)

G MINOR: That's Bass.

(Some cover their own mouths in hopes of convincing G Minor to shut up. Moments later, we hear Bass's secret knock.)

Told you.

A.M.F.M.: Treble, go let Bass in.

DISCO: WaitWaitWait. Treble, stop. We shouldn't open the door. Bass is late.

G MINOR: What's your deal, Disco? Why are you acting so crumpled?

DISCO: When we first met, we came up with rules to protect ourselves. Don't tell anyone your real name. Don't bring anything. Be at the door at your assigned time.

TREBLE: We've never had a meeting without Bass.

DISCO: Because Bass has always been here. On time. I know you all know this, but I feel I always have to remind everyone. If anyone finds out we are here talking about...you know.

G MINOR: Say it. Say "music." Ever since we've been meeting, I don't think I've ever heard you say it.

DISCO: Because I have seen what happens to people who say that word in public.

A.M.F.M.: You may have seen it, but I experienced it. And I'm still not afraid to say it. Mmmmmmmusic.

(Beat.)

DISCO: I'm sorry. I just— It just seems like things are getting worse. Go ahead, Treble.

(Treble exits.)

(Moments later, Treble enters followed by BASS.)

BASS: Thank you for letting me in. I thought about not coming. Because I missed my assigned time. I know. But you know how important these meetings are to me. And I made sure no one followed me. Won't happen again. I promise. And if I break that promise, you do not have to let me in.

DISCO: Why were you late?

BASS: Was at my grandfather's house.

TREBLE: Last meeting, you told us your grandfather died.

BASS: Good memory. And yes. His life did expire. That's why I was at his house today. I was helping my parents clean it out. My grandfather had a pile of bricks in his basement, and he never wanted anyone to touch them. Said he was going to use them but never did. My mom asked me to throw them away.

G MINOR: Ummm...not to sound like I don't care, but can we get back to the meeting? Whose turn is it?

BASS: I promise you will want to hear the rest of my story. So, I'm moving the bricks.

G MINOR: This is so riveting.

BASS: I grab the last one. It looks exactly like a brick but it feels...hollow. I shake it and it sounds like something is in it.

A.M.F.M.: Dead mouse?

BASS: Treble, will you check the door?

TREBLE: I know how to work a lock, Bass.

BASS: Please.

(Treble exits and then returns moments later.)

TREBLE: Locked.

BASS: Close your eyes. Everybody.

DISCO: Why are we closing—

G MINOR: Just do it.

DISCO: OK. They're closed.

(Bass pulls out an object—possibly an iPod, Walkman or phone—and presses a button.)

(Beat as nothing happens.)

BASS: Give me a sec. But keep your eyes closed.

(Bass presses button again. Still nothing.)

You were working earlier.

(Bass presses button a few more times but still no luck.)

DISCO: Can we open our eyes now?

BASS: Go ahead.

DISCO: What in the— You're not supposed to bring anything here. You know that.

TREBLE: What is that you're holding?

BASS: My surprise that doesn't work.

A.M.F.M.: But what is it?

TREBLE: Look at the way G Minor is looking at it.

G MINOR: It's... It's a music player!

(Long beat as everyone scatters away from Bass.)

BASS: Are you sure it's a player?

G MINOR: Saw a picture of one once. My grandfather showed it to me. Before he was taken away.

DISCO: That's a music player?! Oh, we are dead. We are so dead. I knew I shouldn't have come today. I had a feeling this morning. A bad one. And I didn't listen to it. We are soooooo dead.

A.M.F.M.: Disco, will you stop saying that?

DISCO: D.E.A.D.

BASS: It was working earlier. That's why I was late. I was listening to it.

TREBLE: In your grandfather's basement?! What is wrong with you? You know the government has a Listener in every neighborhood. If anyone heard that thing, they are going to report it.

BASS: You should have heard it. It was...it was...no words I use will explain what it felt like in my ears.

DISCO: I want to leave! Now!

A.M.F.M.: Nobody leaves until midnight. That's also one of the rules we came up with.

DISCO: We let Bass in, even though Bass was late. Bass brought something, even though we are not supposed to. Don't tell me about rules.

G MINOR: We are safer in here.

DISCO: I don't want to be silenced.

TREBLE: Nobody made you come here. You came here just like we did. Voluntarily.

DISCO: Because all I thought we were going to do was talk about... That we were going to talk. Tell the stories our grandparents told us. Like we always do.

TREBLE: We could still get sent to the cages for talking about music.

DISCO: Going to the cages is different than being silenced, which is what will happen if we are caught with a music player. I want out!

BASS: If your ears took in what mine did, you would have done the same thing. I wasn't just hearing it. I was feeling it. It's not natural that we are not allowed to listen to music.

DISCO: Music is not worth dying for.

BASS: You wouldn't say that if you actually heard it.

(Beat.)

DISCO: Give me it.

BASS: Why?

DISCO: Give it.

G MINOR: I can see it in your eyes. You want to destroy it.

DISCO: You bet I do.

BASS: I won't let that happen.

A.M.F.M.: Neither will I.

(Disco looks to Treble and G Minor. They join Bass.)

(Long beat.)

DISCO: They. The Silencers. They visited my neighbors last night. The way they pounded on the door. My ears will never forget it. Bang-Bang-Bang! Bang-Bang-Bang!

Someone said my neighbors were hiding instruments in their walls. And it was true. They weren't even taken to jail. They were silenced right there in front of everyone. Things are just getting worse.

TREBLE: If you saw that happen, then why did you come today?

DISCO: Because I didn't want to just not show up.

A.M.F.M.: Others have done that.

DISCO: I know. So I know how it feels. Remember Boombox?

TREBLE: Boombox? You mean Boom?

G MINOR: I totally forgot about Boom.

BASS: In my opinion, the best storyteller.

A.M.F.M.: Boom's grandparents were underground musicians. Even made their own instruments.

DISCO: The day Boom was supposed to show up and tell another story about Grandma and Grandpa Boom, what happened? Boom didn't show. And we don't know what happened to Boom because, well...because we don't know. But I never got to say goodbye. And that might sound too emotional for some of you, but that's what affected me the most. I never got to say goodbye to Boom. And I don't know how much I mean to you all, but you all mean a lot to me. These meetings have meant a lot. And I can't just not show up. I at least have to say goodbye.

BASS: Wait. What are you saying? You're never coming back?

(Beat as Disco shakes head.)

(Suddenly, the music player starts playing.)

(Everyone except for Bass covers ears.)

It works!

DISCO: Turn it off!

BASS: Uncover your ears and let it in. It doesn't hurt. C'mon. Let it in.

(Everyone watches Bass take in the music. Slowly, one by one, the others give in and take in the music. The last is Disco.)

What you are hearing will stay hidden in the folds of your brain until you no longer exist. Even if we never get to hear it again, it will live with us forever. If you start crying, it's OK. I did the same thing when I first heard it.

(The music stops. Silence.)

G MINOR: Why'd you turn it off?

BASS: Didn't. It just cuts on and off like that.

TREBLE: That was...that was...I can't even describe...

G MINOR: Same.

A.M.F.M.: Can we not talk? Can we just...take in the moment?

I'm still feeling things. Things I've never...

(Silence as they all take in what they heard.)

(Moments later, they connect with each other. We see a smile. Hear a laugh.)

(It isn't long before they all hold hands.)

DISCO: Thank you, Bass.

(Disco hugs Bass.)

(Loud banging is heard offstage.)

(Silence.)

A.M.F.M.: G Minor?

(More banging.)

G MINOR: I don't recognize it.

(More banging.)

DISCO: I think...I think they found us.

TREBLE: Who?

(More banging. It's louder than before.)

Who? Who found us?

(The banging continues.)

Who is out there, Disco?

(More banging.)

DISCO: The Silencers.

(More banging.)

G MINOR: How do you know it's them?

DISCO: It's them. It's...them.

(The banging increases. Louder and louder.)

BASS: What do we do?

(More banging. The speed increases.)

DISCO: They are not going to stop knocking.

A.M.F.M.: We continue the meeting. That's why we're here. That's why we came.

(More banging.)

Who's next?

(Blackout.)

(The banging continues.)

(End of play.)

The Author Speaks

What inspired you to write this play?
So many things inspired this play. I've always wanted to write a play that demonstrates my love for music—or is at least inspired by my love for it. Part of my idea for the play was also inspired by the gradual hearing loss I have experienced, probably from driving tanks in the Army. As I thought about my hearing loss, I went from "What if I can't hear music one day?" to "What if there were kids who were never allowed to hear music?" That's just how my brain works.

Was the structure or other elements of the play influenced by any other work?
Before I wrote this play, I read a lot of 10-minute plays. A lot. I wanted to see how other playwrights dealt with slowly revealing information and—what I find most difficult—creating tension in such a short period of time. Two very short plays that helped me were ***Eukiah*** by Lanford Wilson and ***Tape*** by José Rivera. I wanted my audience to experience moments similar to what happens in those plays.

Have you dealt with the same theme(s) in other works that you have written?
No. I've always wanted to write a dystopian/fantasy play. This is mostly influenced by my love for *The Hunger Games* series and the works of Neil Gaiman.

What writers have had the most profound effect on your style?
My writing continues to be influenced by writers of different mediums. I learned how to create vivid imagery from reading poet Martin Espada. Fiction writers Luis Alberto Urrea and N.K. Jemisin's use of magical realism and fantasy continues to influence my storytelling. When I first started writing plays, the works of August Wilson, José Rivera, Suzan-Lori Parks, and the

amazingly talented Anna Deavere Smith showed me how to create stories that matter.

What were the biggest challenges involved in the writing of this play? For example, was there a particular moment that was difficult to write, and if so, why?
All the characters in ***The Day the Music Came Back*** are teenagers. I haven't been a teenager in quite a while, so my hugest challenge was trying to write with the teenage voice in mind. This was also my first time specifically writing a play for teens. I was hoping to create something that would appeal to high schoolers, and at no point in time was it easy. It wasn't until the play was produced and directed by teenagers at Beacon Academy that I felt like I managed to do what I set out to do.

What is your playwriting "origin story"?
When I was a student at Houston Community College, one of the professors asked me to write a TYA play to be performed by the school. I had never written a play before, and I wasn't really into theatre. Yet, the reason I was asked was because I had co-founded a group called Nuestra Palabra: Latino Writers Having Their Say. I'll be honest. I only said "yes" because the professor offered to pay me. $250! My first commission! I went home that night and sketched out some ideas. Within a week, I brought him the play. It was at the first reading of the play that I felt like playwriting was my thing. Hearing those actors bring to life the characters that were in my head was exhilarating. Right there, in that small rehearsal room in downtown Houston, I realized that playwriting was something I wanted to learn more about. The only way I figured to learn more about it was to actually just do it.

How did you research the subject? Are any characters modeled after real life or historical figures?
No research was involved when it came to the subject of the

play. All the characters are fiction and not based on anyone. When creating my characters, I wanted to avoid creating ones that were tropes typically found in some stories geared for teen audiences. Honestly, maybe those tropes don't exist anymore in current stories, but I really wanted to make sure to create characters that felt real and that any teen would love to embody.

What is your writing process?
I'm a morning writer. I usually wake up around 4:00 or 5:00 a.m. That's when my house is really quiet. I'll write a few hours until it's time to start making breakfast for my family. After breakfast, I'll jump back on my computer and write a few more hours. I do this at least three days a week and sometimes on the weekends. If I'm on a deadline, I'll do this five days a week.

Shakespeare gave advice to the players in *Hamlet;* if you could give advice to your cast what would it be?
The only piece of advice I feel I can give relates to the moment when the characters hear music for the first time. I relate it to the first time I heard music that really spoke to me. I hope it might be helpful for each performer to think about that singer or band that woke them up to the possibilities of music. Imagine how it changed your life. That feeling you experienced is connected to the feelings those characters are experiencing.

How was the first production different from the vision that you created in your mind?
One thing I specifically remember that was different was the moment when the characters in the play first hear music. When I wrote it, I envisioned the music to be something by a professional band that maybe the audience had never heard. The key word being "professional," because I assumed whoever was creating sound design would look for something from a Norwegian black metal band or an obscure pianist or something with an accordion. What I didn't think about was the

possibility of using an original piece of music created by one of the teens in the cast. I loved that even more.

When you're not writing, what might we find you doing?
When I'm not writing, I'm teaching playwriting courses at the University of Wisconsin-Milwaukee. If I'm not doing that, I'm reading YA fiction that I checked out from the Chicago Public Library. I usually check out a book a week. Sometimes more. If I'm not doing that, I'm watching YouTube to learn how to cook new recipes. And if I'm not doing *that*, I'm reading folktales and short stories to see what might be worth adapting for the stage.

How did you come up with the title for the play?
The title is inspired by the day known as "The Day the Music Died," a tragic day when the music world lost three talented performers: Ritchie Valens, The Big Bopper and Buddy Holly. I imagined the immense silence their loss created for the teens who loved them and somehow related that to the silence the teens in my play were experiencing. For them, music has been dead for over a hundred years (for devious reasons). But when the teens get an opportunity to hear music for the first time, they are forever changed. And to them, that will always be the day that music came back.

About the Author

Alvaro Saar Rios is a Texican playwright living in Chicago. His plays have been performed in New York City, Mexico City, Hawaii, Chicago, St. Louis, Milwaukee and all over Texas. He has received playwriting commissions from various organizations, including Kennedy Center, Chicago Children's Theatre, First Stage, Houston Grand Opera, Honolulu Theatre for Youth, Purple Rose Theatre Company, Houston Community College, Zoological Society of Milwaukee and Omaha's Rose Theater.

LINDA

by Diana Burbano

CAST OF CHARACTERS

LA LINDA, a young Chicana who might be dressed in a Wonder Woman costume.

TIME

Sometime in the early '80s.

THANK YOUS

Thank you to Andrea Esparza and Sylvia Blush for the first production, and to Lynda Carter and Linda Ronstadt for the inspiration.

(LINDA comes out carrying a box. She is singing a traditional Mariachi song, "Los Laureles," which was on Linda Ronstadt's Canciones de Mi Padre. *She ends with a loud Mariachi cry. She stops, listening. Laughs.)*

LA LINDA: If mi Abuelita was still here, she would've answered back just as loud and we would've danced around the kitchen, using cucharas for castanets until mi papá would yell at us to quit with the tonterías and get him a chela.

I found this stuffed in the closet of mi 'Ita's room.

(She sets down the box which is labeled "Mi Linda". She opens it. Takes out Linda Ronstadt's Living in the USA *record.)*

I wanted to BE Linda Ronstadt. For such a tiny little thing, Linda had such a big sound! I LOVED her god-so-beautiful voice and her cheesy, sexy look. I remember wearing the tube socks and short shorts.

(Pulls a pair of roller skates out of the box.)

My skates! *(Puts them on during the following:)* Que patas tan grandes! I begged and begged for these. I loved to skate around and around our neighborhood on Saturday mornings belting out:

(Sings to the tune of "You're No Good":)

"IN THE HOOD, IN THE HOOD, IN THE HOOD SKA-TIN' IN THE HOOOOOD..."

Until Mr. Gonzalez came out and begged me to stop. He said I was flat. I said, "So was Linda!" He said, "I meant your voice."

"I'LL SAY IT AGAIN..."

(Sings a bit more to Mr. Gonzalez in the audience. We hear a door slam.)

When I was really little I used to confuse La Ronstadt with Wonder Woman. La Mujer Maravilla. She was a Lynda, too.

Lynda Carter! With a Y instead of an I, for fancies. You know, I never missed one minute of that TV show. Not one.

La Wonder Woman gave me hope. Once, in the second grade, I got knocked down by this boy in my class. He'd pull my braids and sit on me like I was a pony. The teachers never did anything. When the bell rang, he whispered "wetback" in my ear. I knew what it meant. At seven years old, it wasn't the first time I'd heard that word.

When I got home that day, I asked my Abuelita what Wonder Woman's golden lasso of truth was made of, and she said she had some of the material in her sewing kit!

I took my lasso to school. I tried to rope the boy, but I ended up whipping him hard in the face with the end of the rope. He told on me to the playground lady. She looked at me all stern at first, and then she smiled! She said, "Good for you, mija. Don't let no boy treat you like crap."

I wanted to be Linda. *(Pronounced Lih-n-da.)* Linda! *(Pronounced Lee-n-da.)* and fierce.

Linda means sexy, tough and in command, not just pretty. Pretty is boring. I bought myself gold Wonder Woman bracelets. At least I thought they were gold until they left big welts on my wrists. That was OK, tho'. I liked the scars. They made me feel tuff, like las Lindas.

(Sings the theme to Wonder Woman *a la "Blue Bayou.")*

"WONDER WOMAN... WHERE THE WORLD IS MINE, WHERE I'M FIGHTING CRIME, ON THE BLUEEEE BAY-OUOOOO!"

Ain't nobody said to either Linda, "Girl, you're asking for it." Cause they weren't! And if you wolf-whistled, you'd get a red boot *(Kicks:)* to the face.

Las Lindas were fly. I put their posters all over my walls. My brothers teased me a lot for not having no boys on my wall like a normal girl, but whatever! I was a Linda! A superhero badass singer who could do whatever I wanted. La Mujer Maravilla.

(She does a little bolero to center stage.)

Abuelita decided that she was going to send me to the "fancy" high school near her work. It had better test scores, better students, no gangs. Yeah—it was white. I stuck out like a little brown sore thumb. Oh, Hera. I was miserable.

Right before Christmas vacation, that first year, I signed up for the school talent show.

The popular girls howled laughing when they saw that. Jerks. They followed me around at recess, teasing me. Telling me to give it up—nobody wanted to see me onstage. I never cried. Never. Amazons don't cry.

I was doing my chores that night, and I THREW the laundry into the basket so hard it made the whole thing flip over onto the floor. 'Ita didn't yell, though. She helped me pick up the basket, made me pan con chocolaté, and we watched her novelas together until I fell asleep.

That was a tough Christmas. The family mi 'Ita worked for made her work late every night. And I don't know where she found the time or the money, but when I opened my Christmas present, Abuelita had made me a Wonder Woman costume. It was nestled in a fancy box from Nordstroms, tissue paper and everything.

I waited to try it on until my brothers were outside trying to kill each other with their new Lawn Darts. I put "Simple Dreams" on the record player, stripped down to my chones, and piece by piece I became la Mujer Maravilla. I put the tiara on my head and—

(She does the Wonder Woman paddle turn and reveals the Wonder Woman costume under her jacket.)

I got super dizzy, but looking at myself in the mirror, I belonged in that superhero costume. This was baby feminista armor.

As Linda hit the last note on "Poor Poor Pitiful Me," a beam of sunshine came in the window and glanced off the tiara. Just like in the TV show! It was a sign. I knew then and there what my talent show act was going to be.

I'd played guitar for years, even though my dad said the guitar was for the boys. I knew I was asking for trouble. Look—all the other acts were basically a bunch of cheerleaders doing stupid dance moves to canned music. Two of them were dancing to "Play that Funky Music, White Boy." Which should tell you all you need to know about my stupid school.

I was #12—really close to the end. I was pretty damn nervous. Had to pee SO BAD, but I couldn't get in and out of the costume in time, so I had to hold it. My turn finally came. I rolled out onstage with my guitar. I toe-stopped, strummed my first chord and sang:

(To the tune of "Blue Bayou":)

"I'M GOING BACK SOMEDAY, COME WHAT MAY, TO PARADISE ISLE—
WHERE THE GIRLS ARE TOUGH, AND BOYS GET ROUGHED UP, PARADISE ISLE—
WHERE I CAN GO— WITH MY LAA-SSOO, AND I CAN CLEARLY SEE,
THAT FAMILIAR SUNRISE, THROUGH TIED-UP GUYS, HOW HAPPY I'D BE."

I got so into it, that at the end I twirled and fell, *(Falls:)* but I played like I'd planned it. *(Plays it off with a* Flashdance *gesture:)* Tada!

I was in a weird DC alternate universe. I knew people were laughing. I heard them. I didn't care. I bowed like I was Linda Ronstadt herself, at a concert in the Hollywood Bowl. Mi 'Ita was clapping like crazy. I looked out, and yeah, it wasn't like I was winning everyone over. This wasn't an ABC Family Movie, where all of a sudden I was accepted for my differences. They were laughing in that mean way kids have. But. BUT. There were actually a few people who seemed to be clapping for real. A teacher I didn't know gave me the thumbs up. Someone's mom was whistling. A cool-looking teen girl was smiling. I saw them. My fellow Amazons. In the sea of mockery I endured for the next six months, I remembered those genuine looks of approval and acceptance, and that fanned a little flame in my soul.

The next year, there was an elective called Xicano studies. With an X. An X! Like X-Men, X. A superhero letter if ever I saw one.

That Xicano Studies class was so intimidating. Holy crap. It took almost till the end of the semester for me to actually speak up in class. But I was listening. I found out so much about myself, about my family. About where I came from, and who I was. I felt like I had been born again.

So, I'm at my friend Tonatzin's house, doing research for a paper my senior year. The topic was, "Latinas in the Media: Spitfire Goddesses and Silent Servants."

Morrissey is on the record player, and Toni puts up a poster that she found at a flea market in Hollywood. It's a collage of faces of Latinos, Hispanics, Mexicans, who had worked in the movies and on TV. I look at it closely. I see Rita Moreno, Rita Hayworth, Carmen Miranda and—I look closer—there, in the middle, about 3 tiny faces apart from each other—there are Linda Ronstadt and Lynda Carter. My heart skips a few beats.

Las Lindas were Mexicanas—my childhood totems, my guide lights. Both of them.

I find out Wonder Woman's real name is Linda Jean Córdova Carter. Linda with an "I." Her mother Juanita was Mexican. And La Ronstadt? It was her dad's side. Dude, Wonder Woman was the ultimate American hero, and she was MEXICAN!!!

(Sings to the tune of the original WW theme song:)

"WONDER WOMAN! FIGHTING FOR YOUR CON-STI-TU-TIONAL RIGHTS!"

I wrote about Las Lindas for my paper instead. When I read it out loud in class, some jerks in my Xicano studies classes were ranking on them, 'cause they were all, like "passing." What did that mean? Passing. Linda Ronstadt put out *Canciones de Mi Padre.* That is a hell of a "This-is-Who-I-Am" statement.

Mi 'Ita—loved what I was discovering. It inspired *her*. She used to joke that she would be the first person from our family to go to college. She really would've blossomed.

(She fights back her tears. Packs up the box and picks it up.)

She was proud of me. The last thing she told me: "Mija, eres la Mujer Maravilla de verdad, verdad." And I said, "No, Abuelita, La Wonder Woman? Eres tu."

(Indicates box.)

She kept my childhood in this box. For me? For herself? I'll never get to ask her.

I got into UCLA, te imaginas? I'm not scared, I'm excited. Maybe there's a girl there who needs to meet a fellow Amazon.

I'm taking my guitar and my roller skates, my gold bracelets and my Abuelita's love. I'm proud of who I am, proud of where

I come from. I'm going to get in my invisible jet, go out over the Blue Bayou and take over the world.

(She ends in a Wonder Woman pose.)

(Lights out. End of play.)

LINDA

(en español)

de Diana Burbano

PERSONAJE

LA LINDA, una joven chicana que podri´a estar vestida con un disfraz de Wonder Woman.

ESCENARIO

En algu´n momento de principios de los 80.

AGRADECIMIENTOS

Gracias a UNAM Universidad Nacional Auto´noma de Me´xico y Lupe Saucedo.

(LINDA sale por la puerta principal llevando una caja. Ella está cantando, "Los Laureles," como Linda Ronstadt en Canciones de Mi Padre. *Termina con un fuerte grito de Mariachi. Para, escucha y se ríe.)*

LA LINDA: Si mi abuelita estuviera aquí, ella hubiera respondido con un gritazo fuerte y las dos hubiéramos bailado alrededor de la cocina, usando cucharas como castañuelas hasta que mi papá nos gritaba "Dejen con las tonterías y tráeme una chela!"
Encontré esta caja debajo de la cama de mi 'Ita.

(Deja la caja. Saca un disco de Living in the USA *de Linda Ronstadt.)*

Guardo mis discos! Yo quería ser Linda Ronstadt. Parecía una muñequita pequeñita, pero Linda tenía una talento enorme! Me encantaba su dios-tan-hermosa voz y su estilo tan super-sexy. Yo me ponía los calcetines de tubo y chores bien cortos, como ella!

(Extrae un par de patines de la caja.)

Mis patines! Uf. Que patas tan grandes! Le rogué a mi papá que me comprara patines para mis 13 años. Los sábados por la mañana, yo patinaba, feliz, alrededor de nuestro barrio,

(Canta con la melodía "You're No Good":)

"IN THE HOOD, IN THE HOOD, IN THE HOOD SKA-TIN' IN THE HOOOOOD..."

El señor González me rogó que "por favor no cante! Estas destemplada!" Por lo menos yo tengo las ganas para cantar, en vez de sentarme en mi pompas y mirar Sábado Gigante todo el día!

"I'LL SAY IT AGAIN..."

(Canta un poco más de "You're No Good" a un Sr. González en la audiencia. Escuchamos un portazo.)

Cuando era muy pequeña, confundí La Ronstadt con Wonder Woman. La Mujer Maravilla también se llamaba Lynda. ¡Lynda Carter! Con "Y" en vez de una "I," por superheroína. Sabes, nunca me perdí un minuto de ese programa en televisión. Ni uno.

La Mujer Maravilla me dio esperanza. Una vez, en el segundo grado, me golpeó este chico en mi clase. Me tiraba las trenzas y se me sentaba encima como si fuera un caballito. Los profesores nunca hicieron nada.

Cuando sonó la campana, susurró: "wetback" en mi oído. Yo sabía lo que significaba. A los 7 años, no era la primera vez que escuchaba esa palabra.

Le pregunté a mi Abuelita qué materiales necesitaba pare hacer Un Lazo de la Verdad como el de la Mujer Maravilla, y ella dijo que tenía ese preciso material en su kit de costura!

Llevé mi lazo a la escuela. Traté de hacerle cuerdas al muchacho, pero acabé azotándolo con fuerza en la cara con El Lazo. Me chismió a la señora del patio. Al principio ella me miró con severidad y luego sonrió. Ella dijo, "Bueno para tí, mija. No dejes que ningún muchacho te trate como mierda."

Yo quería ser Linda. *(Pronunciado Lih-n-da.)* ¡Linda! *(Pronunciado Lee-n-da.)* y feroz. Linda significa sexy, dura y dominante, no solo bonita. Ser bonita es aburrido.

Me compré pulseras de oro a la Mujer Maravilla. Al menos pensé que eran de oro hasta que me dejaron grandes ronchas en las muñecas.
Me gustaron las cicatrices. Me hacían sentir tenaz, como las Lindas.

(Canta el tema a Wonder Woman *a "Blue Bayou" de la Linda R.:)*

"WONDER WOMAN... WHERE THE WORLD IS MINE, WHERE I'M FIGHTING CRIME, ON THE BLUEEEE BAY-OUOOOO!"

Nadie le dijo a las Lindas: "Chica, lo estás pidiendo". ¡Porque no era verdad! Y si silbabas como un lobo, recibirías una bota roja *(Patadas:)* en la cara.

Las Lindas eran magníficas. Puse sus carteles por todas mis paredes. Mis hermanos se burlaban mucho de mí por no tener chicos guapos en mi pared como una chica normal, ¡pero y qué!

Yo era Linda! Un super-héroe badass cantante que podía hacer lo que yo quería. Mujer Maravilla / La Cantadora Dorada!

(Ella baila un bolero al centro del escenario.)

Abuelita decidió que iba a enviarme a la escuela secundaria de "fantasía" cerca de su trabajo. Tenía mejores resultados de pruebas, mejores estudiantes, no había pandillas. Sí—Era para "white people".

Me quedé como un cero a la izquierda. Oh, Hera. Yo estaba miserable.

Justo antes de las vacaciones de Navidad, ese primer año, me inscribí para el show de talentos de la escuela. Las chicas populares aullaban riendo cuando vieron eso. Bobas. Me siguieron en el recreo, burlándose de mí. Diciéndome que lo dejara—nadie quería verme en el escenario. Nunca lloré. Nunca. Las amazonas no lloran.

Estaba haciendo mis tareas esa noche y yo hinqué la ropa en la canasta tan fuerte que bote toda la ropa sobre el piso. My Abuelita no gritó. Ella me ayudó a recoger la canasta, me hizo pan con chocolate, y vimos sus novelas juntas hasta que me quedé dormida.

Fue dura, esa Navidad. La patrona de Ita trabajaba hacía que trabajara tarde todas las noches. No sé de donde encontró el tiempo o el dinero, pero cuando abrí mi regalo de Navidad, Abuelita me había hecho un traje de Mujer Maravilla. Estaba ubicado en una caja de lujo de Nordstroms, papel de seda y todo.

Esperé a probarlo hasta que mis hermanos estaban afuera tratando de matarse unos a otros con sus nuevos dardos de césped. Puse "Simple Dreams" en el tocadiscos. Me desnudé a mis chones, y pieza por pieza me convertí en la Mujer Maravilla. Puse la tiara en mi cabeza y giré, *(hace la vuelta de la pala de Wonder Woman)*. Me mareaba mucho, pero al mirarme en el espejo, pertenecía a ese traje de superhéroe. Era una armadura femenina.

Cuando Linda tocó la última nota sobre "Poor Poor Pitiful Me," un rayo de sol entró por la ventana y relucio hacia la tiara. Al igual que en el programa de televisión! Era una señal. Yo sabía entonces y allí lo que mi acto de espectáculo de talento iba a ser. Había tocado la guitarra durante años, aunque mi padre dijo que la guitarra era para los chicos.

Sabía que estaba pidiendo problemas. Mira— todos los otros actos eran básicamente un montón de animadoras haciendo estúpidos movimientos de baile a la música enlatada. Dos de ellos estaban bailando para "Play that Funky Music, White Boy". Que te dice todo lo que necesitas saber sobre mi estúpida escuela.

Mi turno era #12— muy cerca del final. Estaba muy nerviosa. Tenia que hacer pipí algo horrible! Pero no pude entrar y salir del traje a tiempo, así que tuve que sostenerlo.

Finalmente llegó mi turno. Salí al escenario con mi guitarra. Me paré, toqué mi primer acorde y canté:

(A la melodía de "Blue Bayou":)

"I'M GOING BACK SOMEDAY, COME WHAT MAY, TO PARADISE ISLE–
WHERE THE GIRLS ARE TOUGH, AND BOYS GET ROUGHED UP, PARADISE ISLE–
WHERE I CAN GO– WITH MY LAA-SSOO, AND I CAN CLEARLY SEE,
THAT FAMILIAR SUNRISE, THROUGH TIED-UP GUYS, HOW HAPPY I'D BE."

Me metí en eso, que al final me giró y me caí, *(Se cae:)*, pero jugué como si lo había planeado. *(Juega con un gesto de* Flashdance*:)* Tada!

Yo estaba en un extraño universo DC alternativo. Sabía que la gente se reía. Los escuché. No me importaba. Me incliné como si fuera Linda Ronstadt, en un concierto en el Hollywood Bowl. Mi 'Ita aplaudía como una loca. Vez, no era como si estuviera ganándole a todo el mundo. Ésta no era una película de ABC Family, donde de repente me aceptaron mis diferencias. Se reían de esa manera que los niños tienen. Pero. PERO. En realidad habían algunas personas que parecían estar aplaudiendo de verdad. Una maestra que no conocía me dio el pulgar hacia arriba. La mamá de alguien estaba silbando. Una chica adolescente bien cool me estaba sonriendo. Las vi. Mis compañeras amazonas. En el mar de burla que soporté durante los próximos 6 meses, recordé aquellos genuinos momentos de aprobación y aceptación me daban un poco de llama en el alma.

El próximo año, cumpliendo mi horario de curso, vi una electiva llamada estudios Xicanos. Con una X. ¡Una X! Como X-Men, X. Una carta de superhéroe si alguna vez vi una.

Esa clase de estudios Xicano era tan intimidante. Mi madre! Era casi hasta el final del año para que realmente pudiera llegar a hablar en clase. Pero estaba escuchando. Me enteré tanto de mí mismo, de mi familia. Acerca de dónde vine, y quién era yo. Me sentí como si hubiera nacido de nuevo.

Entonces, estoy en la casa de mi amiga Tonatzin. Estaba haciendo una investigación para un papel en mi último año. El tema era: "Latinas en los Medios de comunicación: Diosas Cacafuegas y Criadas Silenciosas."

Morrissey estaba en el tocadiscos, y aburrida, mire hacia la pared de el dormitorio. Toni, que quería ser la Marilyn Monroe Aztlán pero feminista, había puesto un cartel que encontró en un mercado de pulgas en Hollywood. Era un collage de rostros, latinos, hispanos, mexicanos, que habían trabajado en el cine y en la televisión. Nunca lo había mirado de cerca. Vi a Rita Moreno, a Rita Hayworth, a Carmen Miranda y— Miré más cerca— allí, en el medio, cerca de 3 minúsculas caras aparte una de la otra— Ahí estaban Linda Ronstadt y Lynda Carter. Mi corazón saltó unos golpes.

Las Lindas eran Mexicanas: mis tótems infantiles, mis luces de guía. Ambas.

Descubrí que el verdadero nombre de la Mujer Maravilla era Linda Jean Córdova Carter. Su madre Juanita era de ascendencia mexicana. ¿Y La Ronstadt? Era el lado de su papá.

Dude, Wonder Woman es la mayor heroína americana, y ella era MEXICANA!!!

(Canta a la melodía de la canción de la Mujer Maravilla:)

"WONDER WOMAN! FIGHTING FOR YOUR CON-STI-TU-TIONAL RIGHTS!"

Escribí sobre Las Lindas para mi tesis sobre latinidad en la cultura popular. Cuando leí mi papel, algunos idiotas en mi clase se burlaron, porque ellas estaban "passing." ¿Qué significaba eso? Passing. Linda Ronstadt publicó *Canciones de*

Mi Padre. Eso fue un infierno de una declaración "Esto-es-Quién-Yo-Soy."

Mi Ita leyó todos los libros que traje a casa. Me dijo que ella sería la próxima persona de nuestra familia en graduarse. Nunca lo dudé.

(Ella lucha contra sus lágrimas. Empaca la caja y la recoge.)

Estaba orgullosa de mí. La última cosa que me dijo fue: "Mija, eres la Mujer Maravilla de verdad, verdad." Y yo dije, "No, Abuelita, La Wonder Woman? Eres tu."

(Indica la caja.)

Ella guardó mi niñez en esta caja. ¿Para mí? ¿Para ella misma? Nunca pude preguntarle.

Me aceptaron en UCLA, te imaginas? No tengo miedo, estoy muy emocionada. Tal vez haya una chica que necesite conocer a una compañera amazona.

Estoy tomando mi guitarra y mis patines, mis brazaletes de oro y el amor de mi Abuelita. Estoy orgullosa de quien yo soy, orgullosa de donde vengo. Voy a subir en mi jet invisible, trasvolar por el Blue Bayou y tomar el mundo.

(Ella termina en una pose de Mujer Maravilla.)

(Fin.)

The Author Speaks

What inspired you to write this play?
I loved Wonder Woman so much. She was the ONLY person on TV that I could think of that had black hair like mine. And her name was Diana! As a kid, I was convinced I WAS Wonder Woman and that some supervillain had erased my memory and forced me to take on a somewhat less exciting secret identity than Diana Prince's.

Wonder Woman and Linda Ronstadt were literally the only two women I saw—when I was a little, little kid—that looked anything like me. I never knew why, but I was always super obsessed with them both. And then, like in the play, I saw them in the poster that Nosotros (a Latinx theatre organization in Hollywood) put out to celebrate Latinx in the media. I had NO IDEA that the Lindas were Latinas, and it made me love them even more. Also, I am super goofy and always did very embarrassing things for school talent shows. And suffered for it, but kept doing it nonetheless.

Was the structure or some other element of the play influenced by any other work?
The whole piece is infused with echoes of Linda Ronstadt's great music. And like a lot of memory plays, the music is either misremembered or the lyrics are different. I do feel like the piece might be an old-fashioned record album, and each individual section would be a cut. I love music: I put it in all my work, and I'm happy to say I love all kinds of music: punk, mariachi, klezmer, Phillip Glass. Maybe the only music I've ever found that I didn't want to hear a lot of was yodeling, but I'm willing to give it another chance.

Have you dealt with the same theme(s) in other works that you have written?

Latinidad and erasure and Latinx women are practically ALL I write about in my full-length work. Even if I'm not writing specifically about the theme, I'll always make the characters specifically BIPOC, and even more specifically Latina. I really think that the idea of "any ethnicity" for casting usually means that the BIPOC person is going to play a white character. To try to shoehorn everyone into the same type erases the truth of their lived existence, and I have to push against that idea. Specificity is the key, not "universality."

What writers have had the most profound effect on your style?

Paula Vogel, Tom Stoppard, Octavio Solis, Sarah Ruhl. The Japanese novelists Haruki Murakami and Kazuo Ishiguro are big favorites for style and story. I especially like Ishiguro and Stoppard for examining the countries to which they immigrated. I think everything I write is from an immigrant lens.

What were the biggest challenges involved in the writing of this play? For example, was there a particular moment that was difficult to write, and if so, why?

I think it was really hard to put the word "wetback" in the piece, even though that word was something that actually got thrown around the playground when I was little. I don't even know if a second grader knows what that actually means, what courage it takes to cross a river into a new country that doesn't really want you.

What is your playwriting "origin story"?

I have been a professional working actor since I was 12 years old. I primarily did musical theatre. So, I did the Latinx roles several times, Anita in ***West Side Story***, Rosie in ***Bye Bye Birdie***, the "It's OK to put a Latinx person in these roles" like Mary

Magdalene in ***Jesus Christ Superstar*** and Bianca in ***Kiss Me Kate***. But to be honest, there wasn't a lot that a person who looked like me could do. I transitioned to straight plays and film and TV and, frankly, it just got worse, especially as I got older. I played nannies and cleaning ladies and gang members' mothers. It was exhausting. I was sick to death of being reduced to a one-dimensional stereotype. So I started to write for myself, but then I realized how much joy it gave me to write great parts for other Latinx people. In 2019, my plays gave paying jobs to 36 Latinx performers. That was huge for me and continues to drive me to do what I do.

How did you research the subject? Are any characters modeled after real life or historical figures?
The subject is the life I led, and that lots of other little girls led. Wanting heroines that reflected back upon our lives. Also, I wish I still had roller skates!

These things really happened to me—not quite in the way I've written them, but close enough. The longing to sing out loud, to be a superhero, to make a fool of myself onstage. Discovering what it means to be Latina, and how I'm not alone. All things that I experienced myself.

What is your writing process?
Get up as early as I can, feed the cats, pet the cats, check social media, open Final Draft, look at all the work I have to do, scroll through Twitter, get mad, get coffee, turn on Phillip Glass radio, sit, stare, write a lot of terrible stuff, stare at the terrible stuff, edit, edit, edit, rewrite, coffee, Twitter, write, write faster, fly through writing, four hours later, stop 'cause bum is numb, spellcheck, get annoyed with spellcheck 'cause it's not bilingual, drink water, do yoga, listen to NPR, Japanese on Duolingo, maybe an episode of something funny on TV, but probably not, bed. All the while hanging out with my 14-year-old, feeding

him and myself and my partner, and taking care of his 96-year-old mum.

Shakespeare gave advice to the players in *Hamlet*; if you could give advice to your cast, what would it be?
Your voice is great. You don't have to change your accent. From East LA? Cool! From El Paso? Great! Boricua? Awesome! I love the rhythm of your natural voice! Now, a little louder, and just a titch clearer, make sure we can hear you. Own the way the vowels and consonants land. Own your own rhythm. Don't try and flatten your voice into something archaic and "acceptable." All I ask is that we can hear and understand you. Land it with strength. Your voice is important.

How was the first production different from the vision that you created in your mind?
It wasn't at all! I'm not that attached to the visuals in my work, that's the director and designer's job. I have generally had great outcomes around my work when the people working on them align with my core sensibilities. I had a Latina director and she got it immediately. The actor got it and played and made the character her own. In all the subsequent productions, everyone has interpreted it a little differently, which is exactly what I want.

When you're not writing, what might we find you doing?
Studying Japanese, playing my guitar, singing karaoke, paddle boarding in the Peninsula. Arguing with someone about something. Hopefully rehearsing a play either as a writer or as an actor.

Why is it important that the character identify as Latina?
It's important for the character to come to the realization that she has a history and a narrative that is not the majority narrative. That her family and her people have a rich history,

that it is her responsibility to share that history and that it can come from a place of joy, not trauma. Joy is key.

About the Author

Diana Burbano, a Colombian immigrant, is an Equity actor, a playwright and a teaching artist at South Coast Repertory and Breath of Fire Latina Theatre Ensemble. Diana's plays focus on female protagonists. Plays include ***Policarpa, Fabulous Monsters, Enemy | Flint*** and ***Caliban's Island. Linda*** (in English and in Spanish) has been seen all over the world. Her play ***Ghosts of Bogota*** recently won the nuVoices Festival at Actor's Theatre of Charlotte. ***Ghosts...*** was produced by Alter Theater in the Bay Area. She was in Center Theatre Group'sWriters' Workshop cohort. As an actor, Diana recently played Amalia in Jose Cruz Gonzales' ***American Mariachi*** at South Coast Repertory. Diana is a member of the Alliance of Los Angeles Playwrights. http://dianaburbano.com.

PHANTOM

by Leviticus Jelks III

CAST OF CHARACTERS

MARIA, 16, Latinx, female.

WILL, 16, Black, male.

SETTING

Will's living room. Saturday morning.

CASTING NOTES

Both roles in this play are gender flexible. Character names can be substituted: Maria (change to Marcos) and Will (Willow). The pronouns associated with these characters should be changed as necessary.

Both roles are to be cast only with actors of color, though productions may deviate from the specific ethnicities listed above as needed.

(MARIA, a high schooler, sits uncomfortably on someone else's living room couch. In her hands, she clutches a folded pamphlet, which she opens to read quietly several times. She opens it and reads. She closes it. She opens it and reads. She closes it.)

(Maria hears footsteps on the floor above.)

(She eventually gets up from the couch and begins to pace back and forth, a movement that looks almost trance-like and involuntary.)

(She opens the pamphlet one more time and reads. She takes a deep breath.)

MARIA: *(Exhaling:)* OK...OK. You can do this. You can—you can do this. You have nothing to be…"scared" is not the right word. I mean, he's your friend. I think—No. He is. Don't be...don't be nervous. Yeah. Don't be nervous, Maria. He's still Will *(Chuckles:)* "Still Will," "Still Will"...stupid. OK, focus! ... You got this, Maria. You—

(WILL, another high schooler, walks into the living room.)

(Maria, surprised by someone she was expecting, turns around to see him. She tucks the pamphlet in her back pocket.)

WILL: Hey.

MARIA: ...Hey.

WILL: What're you reading?

MARIA: Huh? What do you mean?

WILL: You just tucked something in your back pocket. Looked intense from the way you were staring it down.

MARIA: ...Oh. That was just something stupid my mom wanted me to read that she got from church.

WILL: Church?

MARIA: Yeah, one of those "How to Save Your Daughter From Going to Hell By Teaching Her Not To Have Sex Before Marriage" things, you know.

WILL: You go to church?

MARIA: You know I got a Holy Roller Catholic mom. You do too. We used to sneak out together and run to the arcade. Got our asses beat every time...don't you remember?

WILL: Oh...oh, yeah. Ummm, you thirsty—?

MARIA: No, I wasn't planning on staying too—

WILL: I can get us some sodas or something—

MARIA: No, no, no. Really, I'm fine.

WILL: OK.

MARIA: Cool.

(Will gestures to the sofa for Maria to sit.)

(She slowly makes her way to the sofa, as does Will, both making sure not to make eye contact.)

(They both sit together. Stiff. Still. Silent.)

WILL: Thanks for coming over.

MARIA: Yeah, sure. I mean, my mom thought it would be a good idea—I mean, I did too. It's just...since she knew we were so close.

WILL: Were?

MARIA: Are?

WILL: Well, don't consider it an act of charity or anything. You didn't have to come over. I know that I'm not exactly your "normal" friend anymore.

MARIA: Well Jesus, what did you expect? None of us are exactly normal anymore after...what happened to you.

(Beat.)

WILL: Sorry.

MARIA: No, it's cool.

WILL: No, it's not. The first person to actually come and see me, and I chew her head off 'cause she didn't come fast enough.

MARIA: To be real, I'm a little relieved.

WILL: Yeah?

MARIA: I mean, people say all kinds of stuff these days. You read stuff online saying that regenerates don't have feelings. Don't get angry. Are just empty meat sacks. It's kind of a relief to get chewed out by you.

(They both laugh.)

WILL: It's just that people don't exactly come around here anymore. My folks won't let me go out. Not without trailing behind me, anyway. I don't blame them. You should've seen the way people looked at me when I first came out.

MARIA: I know. I heard. *(Framing her hands like a newspaper headline:)* "Modern Science Brings High School Teen Back to Life. End of Days or Beginning of the Future?"... Can't say we're all not a little messed up by it.

WILL: And you? How messed up were you?

MARIA: Pretty messed up. I mean, the last thing I heard about you was that they were only able to recover your arm...after the crash. That was all that was left of my friend.

WILL: But it was enough, I guess.

MARIA: Did they ever tell you how long it was?

WILL: ...Six months.

MARIA: Six months. Six months and I had my best friend back. My dead best friend. So yeah, it messed me up, Will.

WILL: Were you happy? When I came back?

MARIA: ...I don't know. I spent six months trying to get past you—I mean, get past what happened to you... Sorry, I know that was a little messed up to say.

WILL: No, that's real. That's what I want. My folks don't show me or tell me anything real.

MARIA: Guess that's their way of protecting you... Parents are stupid.

WILL: Really stupid.

(They both laugh.)

(A beat.)

So...go ahead. Get it over with.

MARIA: What?

WILL: You know. Come on. Let's do this.

MARIA: ...Did you...go to Heaven?

WILL: No.

MARIA: Hell?

WILL: No.

MARIA: ...Anywhere?

WILL: I don't know. I don't remember.

MARIA: Well then, what do you remember?

WILL: I remember when you told me you lost your virginity to Kenny Thomas right on your mom's couch, and how you blamed that stain on your dog and got him taken to the pound. You never talked to Kenny after that. You cried for a week.

MARIA: That was such a bum move by my mom. She never wanted me to have Wilder anyway.

WILL: Or she knew what *really* happened on that couch and wanted to punish you in the harshest way possible.

MARIA: But we got her back, didn't we?

WILL: We sure as hell did. As far as I know she still doesn't know what happened to the velvet Jesus painting.

MARIA: My dad camped out on the couch for a week after that.

(They both laugh. They're getting a little more comfortable.)

(Maria reaches over and her hands hovers over Will's right arm.)

WILL: It's OK.

(Maria touches his arm.)

MARIA: It's so weird. I mean, it's not "weird," it's just—

WILL: I know...

MARIA: Makes me think of Phantom Limb syndrome. When someone loses a limb, sometimes they can still feel it—even when it's not there. But I guess this is the reverse.

WILL: Yeah, I'm the phantom, I guess.

MARIA: No, but you're here, too. At least a version of the "you" that you used to be. Or...*are.* I don't know how it works. It's all just—

MARIA & WILL: So weird.

(Will pulls his arm away. He turns it and flexes it, stretching his hand.)

WILL: At the start, before we get released, all regenerates have to go through this kind of...therapy. Where we sit in front of this..."psychiatric professional." Basically, somebody we don't know, telling us that we're still the real thing. We're still the people who we were.

MARIA: Does that help you?

WILL: Sometimes. But other times I look at this arm. Flex it. Feel it, and I can't help thinking...this is the real Will. This arm. I'm just something that they grew out of it.

(Will puts his arm down.)

(Maria takes out her pamphlet and opens it.)

MARIA: I've been reading this. Picked it up a few weeks ago, after I heard about how you... Says some cool things…

(A beat. Maria clears her throat.)

"Regenerations is dedicated to rebuilding lives and returning what has been lost to families and loved ones"... "A completely safe and painless procedure," yada, yada, yada… "Certified clinicians will conduct a custom re-design of the physical body that is both state of the art and completely organic"—they say "completely" a hell of a lot.

(Will remains silent and still.)

"The new regenerative may not be exactly who they were before, but they will go on to lead a happy and full— "

WILL: Thanks again for coming. I think I need to chill right now. Be by myself. Cool?

MARIA: Cool.

(Maria gets up and begins to walk to the door. She reaches for the knob but hesitates. She begins to shake a little.)

WILL: What is it? You cool?

(Maria takes the pamphlet out of her pocket. She holds it tightly.)

MARIA: You say you remember a lot of things, right? Things that the other Wi—that you knew before...right?

WILL: Yeah, some things. A lot of things, I guess. But they're not really all that clear sometimes.

MARIA: ...What do you remember about that night? The crash?

WILL: I don't wanna do that. I was told not to think about it—my "transition." That's what they call it.

MARIA: I wanna know!

WILL: Well, I don't wanna tell you!

MARIA: ...You remember who was driving?

WILL: *(Getting up from the couch:)* Maria, I don't need to do this right now. Thanks for comin' over.

MARIA: Do you remember who was driving, Will?

WILL: I think I do.

MARIA: Who was it?

WILL: ...

MARIA: And remember when you told me to stop drinking at the party, and you pulled me away? I was so mad at you.

WILL: I was drinking too.

MARIA: But not like I was. Not like me. I knew that if I drove, I'd be screwed, but if my parents saw me pulling up drunk *and* without their car, they'd do to me what they did to Wilder. So, I asked you to drive. I freakin' begged you—

WILL: It's over.

MARIA: I asked my drunk best friend to drive me home. And it killed you. All I walked away with was a broken collarbone. How can that be over?

WILL: I'm right here!

MARIA: Not for six months! For six months I blamed myself, because all I had left of you was an arm. I blamed you at first, you know? Telling myself over and over again that you should've worn a seatbelt or something. That you didn't have to get into the driver's seat. Blaming you for not going home with Sober Steve. He wanted to drive you anyway.

WILL: Yeah, just so he could make out with me. But I didn't want to go home with him. I wanted to go with you.

MARIA: It should've been me. Me *alone*.

WILL: Shut up about it, alright?

MARIA: You remember that night. You remember how scared we both were.

WILL: Yes. I do. Is that what you want to hear? Is that why it took you so long to come and see me?

MARIA: I didn't want to believe it was true. I was hoping that everything that everybody was saying was true. That you all were nothing but empty shells.

WILL: But it's not.

MARIA: When your memory came back, did you hate me? Do you hate me?

WILL: Yes...and yes.

MARIA: *(Taking a deep breath:)* Then why'd you agree to see me?

WILL: I don't know. ... Because you asked. No one else did. And...we were best friends. I don't know if it's still there, but...

MARIA: Cool.

WILL: Cool.

(A beat.)

You wanna watch TV?

(Maria nods.)

(They both walk back to the sofa and sit on opposite ends.)

(Will turns on the TV, and background noise plays.)

(They sit in silence. Maria is still clutching the brochure. She glances over at Will's right arm, holding the remote.)

(End of play.)

The Author Speaks

What inspired you to write this play?

I am a huge sci-fi/fantasy enthusiast, so I love writing plays that have a touch of otherworldly realness against a realistic storyline. The actual inspiration behind the theme of this piece is my wanting to explore the elements of grief, and how they might change if what you were grieving the loss of suddenly came back into your life. I lost a friend in high school to a drunk driver, and I have always wanted to know what I would say to her (or what she would say to me) if she ever came back into my life.

Was the structure or some other element of the play influenced by any other work?

No. This is a pretty straightforward narrative in terms of structure. There is a beginning, a middle and an end. However, I always like to leave a little bit of ambiguity towards the end of my plays. Almost as if we are leaving right in the middle of a conversation, and never got to hear the end of it. The audience is left wondering and asking themselves questions, and I feel it is only when they ask themselves those questions that the magic of the piece truly begins to work. I suppose my inspiration for that is the work of Suzan-Lori Parks, whose plays always have an ending that leaves us wondering.

Have you dealt with the same theme(s) in other works that you have written?

The theme of loss and grief has been a common staple in several of my other works. For instance, in my play, ***Day of Saturn***, the main character, Achilles, deals with the loss of his son due to suicide. Throughout the play, he attempts to reconstruct the moments that led up to the incident by reading his son's old journals.

What writers have had the most profound effect on your style?
I always say that I have the Holy Trinity of writers who influence my work. They are August Wilson, for his narrative style; Tennessee Williams, for the way that he writes such rich and complex characters; also, Suzan-Lori Parks for her fearlessness when it comes to her subject matter and exploration of unusual worlds.

What were the biggest challenges involved in the writing of this play? For example, was there a particular moment that was difficult to write, and if so, why?
When it comes to all of my plays, because they deal with such extraordinary circumstances—or take place in different realities—the challenge of making that world make sense for my audience always presents itself. In terms of this play, I had to convince the audience of a reality where a genetic replica of a person can grow out of a severed limb. While the situation is unusual, I still have to give my audience something concrete to hold on to so they are not spending their focus trying to understand the reality of the piece instead of the plot or the characters.

What is your playwriting "origin story"?
When I was in undergraduate school, I was an English major, but I found out in my last semester that I did not have enough class credits to graduate. So, I had to take a few more classes the following semester, and one of them was playwriting. It was still in the realm of what I wanted to do, but I didn't start out taking it seriously. It was just another elective to take. However, I thoroughly enjoyed being immersed in the world of theatre and writing for it. The first play that I ever wrote, ***The Witch's Fee***, was, in fact, put up for production the next semester. Since then, I have been hooked!

How did you research the subject? Are any characters modeled after real life or historical figures?
The character of Will is modeled after the friend that I lost in a car accident in high school. I researched databases for medical practices which specialize in artificial limbs. I wanted to know how they address their clientele, their language of reassurance and scientific progression. I also researched "phantom limb syndrome" and how it is dealt with by people who have amputated limbs.

What is your writing process?
My basic writing process varies from time to time. However, the way that I usually like to start a play is with an image. I brainstorm different ways that image can be translated into a story, and eventually onto a stage. For example, I have the image of two friends sitting on a couch, and one of them reaches out and touches the other's arm. I ask why they do that and what is happening in that moment. After I dig into that image, then I sketch out my characters and their backstories. Once that happens, I give a loose outline of the play, and after playing with that for a few days, I begin to write the first scene, then the next and on and on until I type those blessed words "End of Play."

Shakespeare gave advice to the players in *Hamlet;* if you could give advice to your cast, what would it be?
No matter what my piece is, I always tell my cast to always be sure to ask questions. By doing this, I feel that all of us learn more about the piece—including me, even though I wrote it. Questions from the actors sometimes give me my best ideas.

When you're not writing, what might we find you doing?
When I am not writing, you can usually find me working as an editor for a bookmaking company. When I am not doing that, I am watching *The Twilight Zone* or reading graphic novels. I also enjoy seeing my friends on the weekends and going to the

beach, weather permitting.

Do the characters in this play have to be gender-specific?
The answer to that is no. I love writing characters who are complex enough where they don't have to be assigned a specific gender.

About the Author

Leviticus Jelks III was born and raised in Atlanta, Georgia. He received a BA in English from Clayton State University, where he also studied theatre and playwriting. He went on to pursue further study of playwriting from The Horizon Theatre as a Playwriting Fellow and The Alliance Theatre as a Literary Intern. Afterwards, he was accepted into the MFA Dramatic Writing program at Carnegie Mellon School of Drama. In his graduate years, he received the Sloan Screenwriting Award for *River Gods* and the Lorraine Hansberry Award for ***A Is for Apron***. His play ***Day of Saturn*** was accepted for a staged reading at the Blank Theatre in Los Angeles, received The Play LA Humanitas Award and will be featured in The Road Theatre Summer Reading Festival. Shortly after moving to Los Angeles, he joined the Los Angeles Playwrights' Union as an official member.

ANATOMY

by Hope Villanueva

CAST OF CHARACTERS

BELLA, white, high school sophomore. Means well, but learning about her own privilege.

ARI, white, high school junior. Willful. Popular and eager to be seen as edgy. Male.

JASMINE, Latina, high school freshman. Gerry's sister. Soft-spoken, wishes she were a bolder person.

GERRY, Latino, high school sophomore. Jasmine's brother. Liked, but doesn't know how to stand up to the group.

KIRSTEN, Asian, high school sophomore. Queen bee of the girl group and captain of the JV color guard.

FRANKIE, Black, high school freshman. Kind, but also unaccepting of injustice. Female.

ROSE, Latina, high school sophomore. Refuses to be walked on.

PRODUCTION NOTES

All the girls belong to the junior varsity color guard. They should be dressed as if it's a warm day at practice, ready to exercise.

Move as quickly as possible between these scenes and keep up pace and energy inside them. These are friends who have a shorthand and speak quickly with each other.

SCENE 1

(GERRY chases down his sister, JASMINE, as she exits school and walks home.)

GERRY: Jasmine, wait!

(Jasmine stops, shoots daggers, then whips around to keep walking.)

Hey, no, wait!

JASMINE: Screw off, Gerry.

(Gerry manages to get in front of her.)

You're dead. When I tell Mom—

GERRY: You can't!

JASMINE: I had no idea that you could—

GERRY: It was just a goof. For our friends.

JASMINE: That "goof" is playing on every cell phone at every break—

GERRY: Don't tell Mom.

JASMINE: Are you kidding me?

GERRY: I've got an away game this weekend! And there's—

JASMINE: She should ground you! Mom is gonna lose her—

GERRY: Look, please. Mom doesn't need to find out. She hates social media, so she'll never see... unless you tell her.

JASMINE: Are you kidding?!?

GERRY: Please, Jasmine. Jas. Please. I never ask you for anything. I'm your brother.

JASMINE: You messed up.

GERRY: Yeah.

JASMINE: I shouldn't cover for you...

(She's caving just a little... But still hurt.)

GERRY: Thank you! Jas, you're saving my butt!

JASMINE: Yeah, fine. But know that you deserve whatever Mom would have done.

GERRY: Cut me some slack!

JASMINE: Half the football team was hooting at me when I left gym today 'cause of your stupid video. You really don't get it!

(Jasmine storms away.)

(Jump to the video: A basement. Gerry and his friend ARI are talking into the camera, careless with their actions and words.)

GERRY: *(Laughing:)* Naw, dude. Bad idea.

ARI: Just for our friends. It'll be hilarious. Come on!

(A doubt. And then –)

GERRY: Okay. Yeah –

ARI: Woo! Go back to the top of the list. You filming? Okay, okay, okay... Starting with the JV Color Guard...

(Gerry pulls up photos on his phone and indicates the pictures as he and Ari talk.)

GERRY: Should've started with the cheerleaders. They're hotter.

ARI: What? Look at Kirsten. Asian girls are not usually my thing, but I'd make an exception. How's she always running around in those tiny shorts?

(The video keeps playing... A group of friends – ROSE, FRANKIE, KIRSTEN and BELLA – are watching on one of their cell phones. Bella looks to Kirsten at the mention of her name.)

BELLA: Kirsten...

ROSE: Are you kidding?

FRANKIE: What the—?

ARI: I'd do her for sure. For sure.

GERRY: Kirsten's Color Guard captain. Of course she's hot.

ARI: I give Kirsten...a nine.

GERRY: NINE!

(The guys laugh. The girls cringe.)

ROSE: What do you think of Ari now, Bella?

BELLA: But he's always been so nice to me.

KIRSTEN: To your face.

(Back to the video:)

ARI: Rose? Serious?

GERRY: Oh yeah. She's at least an eight, but the way she walks, those hips—

ARI: She wore that tiny denim skirt to the Spring Picnic!

GERRY: It's like, she sways. Those hips.

(Ari gestures like he's grabbing onto choice body parts.)

ARI: I just wanted to— Like I totally could have—

(Ari grabs the phone from Gerry and licks the digital picture of Rose. Gerry dies of laughter, but the girls recoil in disgust.)

GERRY: *(Cracking up:)* You're gonna ruin my phone, dude!

(Frankie snatches the phone away. Jasmine walks up to the group.)

FRANKIE: How do we block—

JASMINE: Can we please just not with that video? Not when we're together—

BELLA: I can't believe Ari.

KIRSTEN: I can. Look—I didn't want to burst your bubble about Ari, but he's a jerk.

BELLA: He helped me with my history assignment. Just last week.

KIRSTEN: Do you remember what shirt you had on that day?

(Bella shakes her head. Kirsten pushes her arms and shoulders forward to indicate "cleavage.")

BELLA: That wasn't— No!

JASMINE: Sorry, Bella.

FRANKIE: *(From aside:)* Oh, they just keep going—

ROSE: I saw it on Christina's page in sixth period and Lawrence totally shared it. It's on Paul Johnson's Insta. If he has it... *(Unsaid: Everyone has it.)*

FRANKIE: We have to tell somebody.

KIRSTEN: It's a stupid video. So what.

BELLA: It's not like they broke the law—

FRANKIE: You're cool with them talking about you?

(Frankie holds up the phone and hits play again. The boys reappear.)

GERRY: Hell yeah!

ARI: Bella filled out that tank top like—

GERRY: Wooo!

(Stop video. Frankie waits. Kirsten tries to cool the situation down.)

KIRSTEN: Let them look.

JASMINE: Kirsten, don't you feel...violated?

ROSE: You should.

KIRSTEN: Who are we gonna tell? It's a free internet.

SCENE 2

(Gerry and Ari are playing video games a week later. They hit the end of a level and pause. Gerry grabs more soda from nearby.)

ARI: I'm outta practice after a week in solitary. I'm getting back in my groove.

GERRY: Only a week—

ARI: My stupid brother saw and gave me up.

(They drink.)

Dad didn't actually care. But Mom made a stink about me learning a lesson and blah blah blah.

GERRY: Our Mom doesn't know.

ARI: How'd you pull that—

GERRY: I begged Jasmine. Begged. But like... I dunno. Like, Jas was really upset.

ARI: It was just laughs. You had fun, right?

GERRY: Yeah.

ARI: You both need to relax. In a week, no one will remember. Besides, you "meant" all the stuff you said.

GERRY: No, I—

ARI: You've had a mad crush on Frankie since middle school. And everyone thinks Kirsten is hot. 'Cause she is. Everything in the video is true.

GERRY: I guess so. Jasmine is probably overreacting.

ARI: Man. Can we just play this game?

(They get back into it.)

SCENE 3

(Jasmine, Frankie, and Bella are hanging out in the hall.)

JASMINE: It's been over a week, and people are still looking at us.

BELLA: What else do you want? Ari did his time.

JASMINE: Do you hear yourself?

FRANKIE: That's part of the problem. "Did his time"?

JASMINE: You and I both know Ari doesn't care about that.

FRANKIE: I told Ms. Rushland.

BELLA: What? Why?

FRANKIE: She caught someone in class watching and took their phone and...yeah. She was like, "It didn't happen at school." And "I wish there was something more I could do." She said things like that just keep on happening in college and stuff. "Frankie," she says, "there's men like that everywhere, and you have to learn to walk past." This is some bull...

(Kirsten and Rose join them from a nearby classroom.)

KIRSTEN: Frankie, you still pissed about this?

FRANKIE: Maybe you all should be madder about it.

ROSE: Being mad is making me tired. Then, I get mad about being mad making me tired.

FRANKIE: I still can't believe you covered for Gerry.

JASMINE: Me either. But he's not really like that—

BELLA: Neither is Ari.

KIRSTEN: *(Sarcastic:)* Sure.

(Ari and Gerry move down the hallway, past the girls.)

GERRY: Barely made it through that one. Chem will end me.

ARI: But you passed.

GERRY: Coming over today?

(Gerry gives him a shove and they laugh, but freeze when they see Rose, Frankie, and squad glaring in their direction.)

(They all eyeball each other. Gerry and Ari start walking again, but as they pass, Ari whispers in Kirsten's direction:)

ARI: Heeey, Legs.

GERRY: *(To Ari:)* Shut up!

(Kirsten turns squarely to face Ari and Gerry.)

Hey. Ari's a moron. Just ignore...

(Kirsten clearly has the upper hand. She gets really close to them, almost sniffing them. Gerry tries to hold his ground.)

Give it a few more days and something else is gonna come through TikTok or IG or...

(Gerry is out of steam. Kirsten spins away in disgust. Frankie laughs, and Rose scowls. Kirsten leading, the girls continue walking.)

(They're almost clear when Ari makes a lewd gesture in their direction. It's enough to catch Rose's eye. The girls stop in their tracks when Rose does.)

GERRY: We're dumb. Don't—

ARI: I mean, if you can't take a joke—

(Rose punches Ari in the gut. Ari hits the ground. Gerry drops to him, and Frankie and Kirsten pull Rose away.)

ROSE: You had that coming!

(The girls are gone. As Ari is catching his breath, the school bell rings.)

SCENE 4

(Kirsten and Rose have been taken to one administrator's office, Gerry and Ari to another.)

(All vent directly to their respective unseen authorities unless otherwise noted.)

ARI: That crazy little— *(He smothers what he wants to call her:)* She punched me out of nowhere!

KIRSTEN: Everyone's seen it.

ROSE: The whole school!

GERRY: Okay. Yes, we did make that video—

ARI: *(To Gerry:)* Don't make it sound like we did anything wrong!

GERRY: We didn't know everyone would be so upset—

KIRSTEN: These two jerks—

GERRY: We shouldn't have said all that.

ARI: Not like we hurt anybody. But Rose— I think she broke my rib—

GERRY: *(To Ari:)* Rose didn't break your—

(Ari makes as if he's in pain, but he's clearly okay.)

KIRSTEN: It's all like... These idiots want to say whatever, I don't care. I know what's real. I got in their faces, mostly 'cause I want them to know that I know, right?

ROSE: You can't just come for my friends and not expect—

GERRY: It was a game. It was stupid.

ARI: It was only supposed to be for a few friends.

ROSE: I'm glad! He deserved it, and I'm not sorry!

(Just outside the offices where their fellow students are being grilled, Bella, Jasmine and Frankie wait... This action takes place as the two office scenes continue.)

BELLA: They going to get suspended?

FRANKIE: Doubt it—

JASMINE: Gerry's never even had a detention.

FRANKIE: Why do you two want to make excuses? Like they don't suck when they obviously suck? Besides. Nothing's gonna happen.

(Back inside the administrator's offices, Rose is getting fired up.)

ROSE: Detention? That's all they get?

KIRSTEN: Yeah, then they'll go home to their video games and laugh about how lame you are.

ARI: This is so lame!

GERRY: *(To Ari:)* You know that this was more than a little wrong, right?

ARI: There's no rule—

GERRY: Why am I even sticking up for you? Some stuff is wrong just 'cause it is.

ROSE: Me? You want to suspend me?

KIRSTEN: Rose was super provoked. You have to at least suspend Gerry and Ari, too.

ROSE: Or how about NOT suspending me?!?

(The administration offices begin to fade into the background.)

(Outside the offices, in the hall, Bella's been trying to make a case to her friends—)

FRANKIE: What matters is Rose threw a punch. The guys will just...be guys. Gerry will have Ari's back, 'cause he's done that since kindergarten. He thinks 'cause Ari's popular that it'll rub off. And Ari's, you know.

(She lets it hang as if they know... Jasmine nods. But Bella –)

BELLA: Ari's what?

FRANKIE: I mean... He's white.

BELLA: But... I don't want him to – but – it's not –

JASMINE: Why are you...? 'Cause he gave you the time of day for five seconds? You can't give Ari a pass 'cause you wish he was a good person.

FRANKIE: Ari'll get the benefit of the doubt. Gerry, too. But Rose is in trouble.

(Back in the admin office, Kirsten consoles Rose, who is losing it.)

ROSE: I don't care if you suspend me! I don't want to walk down the hall and wonder if they saw the video. Nobody looks at my eyes since – I can't walk from bio to history without – Gerry was worried about Ari drooling on his phone. A cell phone matters more than – Why does anybody get to say any crazy thing about what I look like – but what about me just being a person?!?

ARI: *(Calmer now:)* Yeah. Okay. But she punched me.

GERRY: Dude! Are you even sorry? What's wrong with you?!?

(Outside:)

BELLA: Am I just supposed to assume everyone is – every guy is bad?

JASMINE: We can't assume they're good.

FRANKIE: It's like being a girl is a trap. If we fight back, we're punished. If we don't, they'll just...to us.

JASMINE: So what then? How does it stop?

(Jasmine, Bella, and Frankie exchange a silent, weighty thought.)

(End of play.)

The Author Speaks

What inspired you to write this play?

Anatomy was inspired by a real incident. I work with a musical theatre group that is founded and led by high school students. We had a male student who is on the autism spectrum, and we discovered that he had been keeping a list of the girls in the company and rating their bodies. Not understanding the social cues or boundaries, he decided to share this information with a girl he seemed to like. She asked him to stop and to leave her alone, but when he didn't, the company decided to ask him to exit (after consulting his parents). It was a stressful and complicated situation, and the resolution felt like the right choice and somehow unsatisfying at the same time. His leaving didn't erase the incident from having happened or stop the girls on that list from feeling objectified. But really, it's just a micro version of the kind of physical judgment that's common in the entertainment industry and in society. It's not the first time I've encountered something like this, and it always makes me furious that anyone could think this is alright to do. I tried to funnel those complex feelings into this piece.

Was the structure or some other element of the play influenced by any other work?

There wasn't anything consciously influencing the structure of this play, though I often explore multiple threads or narratives in my pieces. It was important to me that I represented a number of different reactions in the girls' friend group, based on their individual viewpoints. I also wanted to include the view of the boys who made the video, not really understanding how harmful what they were creating was. The ending of the play, with the two parallel rooms of administrators, was meant to reflect the futility of the adults in the teens' lives in this Wild West of modern social media.

Have you dealt with the same theme(s) in other works that you have written?
I don't usually have characters in my play that are this actively angry or who get physically violent, so these are some new elements for me. I do include teenaged or early adulthood characters in my pieces, since I recall those years as a time in life when I was making big decisions about who I was and what I wanted to do with my life—so the stakes of every day, every friendship, every choice felt heightened. Higher stakes lend themselves to the theatrical.

What were the biggest challenges involved in the writing of this play? For example, was there a particular moment that was difficult to write, and if so, why?
The hardest part of this piece was trying to tamp down the level of vulgarity for this to be school-appropriate. As someone who does work with high schoolers, they are just on the edge of being adults and regularly push that boundary when they are among their friends or people they trust. They don't want to be treated like children or be spoon-fed ideas. I know that in the real-life version of this story, there would be a ton more swearing, and the actions from the boys in the video could be much, much grosser. But I also knew that teachers and parents wouldn't likely let their students do a play that was written with that level of cursing and vulgarity.

In particular, finding the physical action taken by Ari or Gerry in the video was hard. I contacted some of my trusted play reader friends—some of whom are younger than I am—to look. We ended up getting on a Zoom call together and bouncing around our favorite bad pick-up lines and gross frat boy gestures. I can't share them here, but it got really animated! Then we looked at how we could pull back just enough to get past the internal censors of adults and still get the visceral reaction from the girls watching. I hope I stuck the landing on that.

What is your playwriting "origin story"?
I was a dancer when I was young and quit when I got to college—after being told by my parents that the arts were not a career. I was doing well as a biology major but found myself growing more unsatisfied and unfulfilled. On an impulse, I signed up for a playwriting course my junior year and loved it. I completed the entire playwriting series and changed my major to theatre at the start of my senior year, still graduating on time. After leaving school, my playwriting fell by the wayside for a number of years as I ventured into assistant directing and stage management, which is how I still make almost all my living. It wasn't until nearly a decade later, when one of my artistic directors encouraged me to write a short for a production, that I found my way back to playwriting, and I've been writing ever since.

What is your writing process?
I'm a big believer in the collaborative process in theatre. My initial drafts are a very private project where I try to just let whatever wants to come on out. I used to outline but find that in the early phase it stunts my flow. Once I have a full first draft, I start enlisting trusted friends to read it and give me broad notes about clarity and character. I often find that once I get to know the people, the rest of the play starts shaping itself. After a few passes—it usually takes three to five drafts—I feel a bit more comfortable and may try to assemble a reading or put the work into the hands of a producer I trust. Typically, I won't start submitting anything until its sixth or seventh draft. Of course, for this piece, which had a prompt and tight timeline, I simply had to set deadlines for myself and just press forward.

Shakespeare gave advice to the players in *Hamlet;* if you could give advice to your cast, what would it be?
Play each character as a complete, real person, with a full

spectrum of emotions. No character in this play is entirely one note. Even Ari as the "villain" of the piece rides an arc as he hits the inciting incident and lives through the fall out.

What do you want people to leave this play feeling?
Anatomy could easily have gone into what actually happens in terms of the students being punished or not punished, but I felt like focusing on the emotion was more important than what actually happens. I wanted to touch on all the different feelings the girls touch on—disbelief, shock, futility, disgust, anger, vulnerability, etc.—and raise those up. I also wanted to note that it's possible for a boy to take part in a bad decision like the creation of this video and also regret what he's done afterwards. I also wanted to examine how influential social media is and what an emotionally unsafe terrain it can be when used carelessly. It was never my goal to provide answers to these questions, but rather to put the audience in a position where they walk away from the play and are talking about those issues as they're having dinner after the show.

About the Author

Hope Villanueva is an AEA stage manager by profession but constantly writes. She was a 2021 O'Neill Finalist, and her work has been presented at New Works Virtual Festival, Kennedy Center Page to Stage, Ally Theatre Company, Next Stop Theatre, The Women's Voices Theatre Festival, Next Act! New Play Summit, the Baltimore Playwrights' Festival, The Black and Latino Playwrights' Conference, The Discovery New Play Festival and Kitchen Dog New Play Festival. Her play, ***Her, Across the River,*** was part of the INKubator On Air and can be heard on iTunes and Spotify, and ***The Veils,*** was audio recorded for The Parsnip Ship. She is the Literary Manager at Bay Street Theatre in Sag Harbor, NY

THE MASK ON THE BENCH

by Ramiz Monsef

CAST OF CHARACTERS

JACKSON, African-American, 17, male.

KARIM, Middle Eastern, 17, male.

(A tiny bedroom in a tiny apartment in a city somewhere in America.)

(JACKSON [17, African-American] is watching an old horror movie on an old TV. There are records and comic books strewn about.)

(The movie blares, but Jackson isn't listening. He has his headphones on and is making a beat on a little sampler. An SP-404 kind of thing. He gets frustrated with what he is doing and rips his headphones off. He gets sucked into the movie for a moment.)

WOMAN IN MOVIE: No, Richard. Don't come any closer. Your face it's...it's hideous. What have you done to your face?

MAN IN MOVIE: I made a wish. That's all I did! I made a wish! What's happened to me??

WOMAN IN MOVIE: Oh Richard. You...you need to stay away from me! Stay away!!!! Nooooo!!!!

(Jackson's phone rings.)

JACKSON: Karim, what's good, man? You alright? Why you sound so out of breath? Where are you, man?

(A face appears in Jackson's window.)

(Jackson turns and sees it. It spooks him and he jumps.)

What the—

(KARIM [17, Middle Eastern] opens the window.)

KARIM: What I tell you about watching those movies at night?

JACKSON: What I tell you about climbing the fire escape? You know Raoul got a shotgun one floor down, right?

KARIM: I know.

JACKSON: So, you think you some kinda master thief? You gonna dodge security lasers *and* buckshot?

KARIM: Yo c'I come in or what?

JACKSON: What are you, Dracula? You need an invitation? You already scaled the building. Come on up in this house.

(Karim cautiously crawls through the window. He holds his backpack like it contains precious cargo.)

KARIM: Your moms asleep?

JACKSON: Yeah.

KARIM: Word. Manny?

JACKSON: He passed out. You know that old drunk can't keep his eyes open past 9:30 and a fifth of Seagram's. Wack-[ass] stepdad.

KARIM: Ok word.

JACKSON: Wassup? You look like you just found the Ark of the Covenant or something.

KARIM: Yeah yo. Kinda. Yo, yo, crazy.

JACKSON: What's in your bag? Nobody followed you or nothing, right? You look mad guilty. What did you do?

KARIM: I didn't do anything! I just put it on! And-and...

JACKSON: Put what on?

KARIM: Check it.

(Karim opens his bag, and both he and Jackson look inside. A golden light emanates from within.)

I found it on a bench in the train station.

JACKSON: Whhhhhhaaat is that?

KARIM: It's a mask.

JACKSON: I know it's a mask but—

(Jackson tries to touch it.)

KARIM: Don't touch it!

JACKSON: Yo, ease up. What's your problem B? You coming in here like someone's chasing you.

KARIM: That's 'cause they might be.

JACKSON: Who?

KARIM: ...Chup. Well not Chup, but his people...

JACKSON: Chupacabra? Yo, get out of my house. I don't want that fool or any of his goons knowing where I live! That guy is mad dangerous B!

KARIM: You think I don't know that? But yo listen, this mask...I found it at the station. It was just sitting on a bench.

JACKSON: You said that.

KARIM: Yeah but you don't understand. It was like it was waiting for me. Like it put itself there.

JACKSON: Is that metal? Is it moving?

(Shakes his head in disbelief.)

I've never seen anything like it.

KARIM: Yeah. And it's weird—it's like the more you look at it, the less you can understand what it is you're seeing.

JACKSON: Yeah...waaaaait...you high?

KARIM: Look in my eye.

(Jackson does.)

JACKSON: Ok. So we serious.

KARIM: Super serious. Yo peep though. I found it, right? I pick it up. It feels mad heavy right? Like heavier than it looks. And I see on the inside, it's glowing. Crazy.

JACKSON: Crazy.

KARIM: You know me. I'm the curious type, so I put it on right? And yo, the whole time, walking to the train station, I'm freestyling in my head, like I always do, but the rhymes are wack tonight for some reason. Can't focus. Can't grab any references, just sorta floundering with the same old party rocks like, "Oo I'm so tight/clutch the mic/strike lightning/the kind of MC who so frightening/Now check the math/I got codes hidden in sentences and paragraphs." Wack stuff. Old stuff. But then I see the mask, right? Put it on. And like the whole world changes. It's like I'm surfing words. Like I'm floating above them and I can see the absolute best one for every line. All of a sudden I got mad punchlines flowing through my head, like I can't stop. Like I'm the long-lost son of Supernatural. It's unreal!

JACKSON: Whoa.

KARIM: But then I hear this voice. Like, "AY!" I turn around, and guess who's standing there. One guess.

JACKSON: Chup?

KARIM: Nail on the head. Chupacabra.

JACKSON: Man that dude always shows up at the WORST times. It's like he KNOWS when you got something worth taking.

KARIM: Word. Like a sixth sense. Remember when I copped those Jordans and the same DAY, Chup shows up in the cypher, spits a couple bars, and then takes one look at me and is like, "I like your shoes." I knew right then I'd be walking home in socks.

JACKSON: The man is a public menace. And he's a terrible MC! Always spitting the same 16's. Like we KNOW that ish is written!

KARIM: Yeah well, there he is. Seeing I got something he wants. And I don't know what came over me. I mean I had the mask on and it was giving me this...confidence. So I look at

Chup and I'm like "Naw." In fact, "Hell naw." And he gets this look in his eyes like he never heard that before. Like the word "NO" was some kinda alien language. And then I don't know what came over me...

JACKSON: What?

KARIM: For real J. I looked at him...and I spit the illest verse I ever spit in my life! It was like words were shooting out of my mouth and the mask, the mask was TELLING me what to say yo!

JACKSON: What was the verse??? Spit it!!

KARIM: Yeah word it was...uh...it was...I can't remember it yo!

JACKSON: You gotta be kidding me.

KARIM: I wish I was 'cause, yo, as I was spitting, it was like each bar was pushing Chup just a little further back. Till the backs of his feet was just hanging over the edge of the platform. And—

JACKSON: What—

KARIM: And I got to the end of the verse and, I don't even know what I said but I came with this punchline that was half punchline and half Hadouken. It wasn't me! It was the mask and the words! They— And I *saw* the train coming and I couldn't stop rhyming. I had to finish, but my words were *pushing* him. I saw what I was doing and I saw the train and—

JACKSON: Naw.

KARIM: Chup ain't gonna be bothering anyone anymore.

JACKSON: Whoa.

KARIM: Yeah.

(A beat as they both look to Karim's bag which holds the mask.)

JACKSON: Look, I never liked Chup, I mean, no one really liked him. Guy was a menace, and a bully, and he had that nasty milk breath and he'd always make a point of getting extra close to you when he wanted to scare you just so you smell it. Buuuuuuut...

KARIM: Yeah, I know. Look I don't feel good about it either. In fact, I've been feeling kinda nauseous and, I don't know...panicked, since it happened.

JACKSON: I guess I would be too.

(Looking at the backpack again:)

And you just...put that on?

KARIM: Yeah.

JACKSON: And you became a real life Supa MC.

KARIM: Yeah, SUPA in ALL CAPS. It's like the mask gives you what you want, but it takes something in return.

JACKSON: Word. Well, we both know ain't nothing free in this world. Anyone see you?

KARIM: I don't think so. Whoever was on that train got a pretty nasty show though. It was like...

(Mimics the sound of a big messy explosion.)

(Then a beat.)

Yo...what do we do???

(Jackson is staring at the bag now. Drawn to its power.)

JACKSON: You have literal killer bars now.

KARIM: Not me! The mask!

JACKSON: What if...what if this mask belonged to, like, some kind of evil supervillain, or like someone who *called* themselves a villain, but who was more of an antihero type, and like, he died, but he didn't want his legacy to die too, so he left this mask on a bench for the *next* supervillain to pick up so they could carry on his...vibe.

KARIM: You been reading too many comic books yo.

JACKSON: Word...hey um...lemme try it on.

(Jackson reaches for Karim's bag.)

KARIM: What? No!

JACKSON: Come on, Karim! I been messing with this beat for HOURS. I can't get it to knock right. I've tried everything, but the snares sound tinny and I can't get the kick to give me the right BOOM.

KARIM: So try harder! 10,000 hours, homie! We both knew the rap game wasn't easy.

JACKSON: Come on! I'm stuck bro, and you got a wearable *Limitless* pill in your bag! Think about it, I put that mask on and make you some beats, then you put it on and write the rhymes, and then we can get our own spot-slash-studio, and I won't ever have to deal with drunk Manny again!

KARIM: Trust me. You don't want this. It won't fix anything.

JACKSON: This could be what puts us over!

KARIM: What?

JACKSON: Think about it. K-Mack and J-Boogie. Killing it.

KARIM: Yeah. For real killing.

JACKSON: Last show we played, audience was like zombies, man. No one cared.

KARIM: No one cared because we were playing a "show" next to a cell phone kiosk in the mall!

JACKSON: No one cared because we weren't very good dawg. We need this mask. Put it on and be the MC you were always meant to be. Or let me wear it and I'll be the Primo to your Guru. Think about it...

(Karim does for a moment.)

KARIM: Naw. That's not what K-Mack and J-Boog are about. And you didn't see Chup. That train. I mean, he went everywhere. Naw. Like, I know nothing that makes you feel that powerful can be good for you in the long run. It's gotta cost something. And I don't want to wait around long enough to find out what. Naw. If I'm gonna be a SUPA MC it's gonna be 'cause I worked on it. Me. I practiced. Naw. I'm about to go throw this mask in the river. No one should be able to feel this kinda power. I'm shook J. Straight up. I may never rap again. Not if it does that! I just needed to stop by to, like, regroup and catch my breath. This was the only safe place I could think of that was even kind of nearby. I mean, nobody liked Chup, but dude had some clout. There's people gonna be upset something happened to him.

JACKSON: Ok word. And you sure no one followed you?

KARIM: Yeah.

JACKSON: Positive.

KARIM: Absolutely.

JACKSON: Naw. Check.

KARIM: What?

JACKSON: Check outside yo!

KARIM: I did!

JACKSON: Well check again!

KARIM: What about Raoul with the shotty?

JACKSON: Man, Raoul blind as a cave fish. Check! I don't want nunna Chups goons coming up in here.

KARIM: Aiight fine! Be right back.

(Karim dips back out the window to check.)

(As soon as he leaves, Jackson grabs Karim's backpack and runs into the bathroom. From within the bathroom a glow emanates. Jackson, needing to move quickly, runs back out of the bathroom with the backpack now empty, and replaces it with a book wrapped in a t-shirt or something. He puts the backpack back where it was.)

(IMPORTANT: WE DO NOT EVER SEE THE MASK.)

(Karim comes back in.)

Coast is clear. I told you.

JACKSON: Yo, you gotta dip! I just heard Manny. He comin', and you know we can't let him get his sloppy hands on this thing.

KARIM: Aiight bet. Good lookin out. Yo, I'm tossing this thing.

JACKSON: Fine! Toss it, but you gotta go yo!

KARIM: I'm out. I'm gone.

(Karim grabs his bag and dips out the window. Jackson watches him a moment and then runs into the bathroom. The familiar glow emanates.)

(Then –)

(Karim pops his head back in the window.)

Yo!

(The light in the bathroom immediately goes out. Jackson comes out.)

JACKSON: What? You gotta stop scaring me like that!

KARIM: Sorry yo, but-

JACKSON: What??

KARIM: Downstairs. Raoul. His light is on. I don't know what to do.

JACKSON: I told you the dude is blind. You're fine. Just be quiet! I tell you what, you gonna have problems right here you scare me like that again.

KARIM: My bad J, I just...Raoul with the shotty.

JACKSON: Blind as a bat that hates carrots. I told you. Go.

KARIM: Aiight. Aiight. K-Mack and J-Boog.

JACKSON: K-Mack and J-Boog.

(They fist bump.)

KARIM: We good?

JACKSON: Yeah we good. Now dip. I swear Manny gonna come in here any second!

KARIM: I'm out!

(Karim exits.)

(Jackson waits a moment this time. Then he slinks into his bathroom again. The glow returns. It burns brighter this time. Brighter. Then –)

(BANG!)

(We hear a shot from downstairs.)

(The glow goes out.)

(Jackson runs to his window.)

JACKSON: Karim!

(Nothing.)

KARIM!

(Still nothing.)

Naw.

(Jackson crumples by the window, wrestling with the consequences of his actions.)

(End of play.)

The Author Speaks

What inspired you to write this play?

I've been writing a lot of horror lately. I guess that's just where my creative brain has been at. I mean...2020 was...a year. But also I love the genre. I love how it has a specific build, and good horror has good rhythm. I'm a drummer, so rhythm is important to me. Also, when MF DOOM died I wanted to write something that had the essence of his immense influence on the culture. So his spirit is in there. I almost don't even want to talk about it and leave it to the young performers to dig deeper if they want to...Easter eggs, ya know? Also, I love the idea of being able to write something that I would have wanted to do as a young actor.

Was the structure or some other element of the play influenced by any other work?

Loosely yes. In addition to loving classic boom-bap hip-hop, I also am a big nerd for the old horror mags from the '60s and '70s. *Creepy* and *Eerie* and *Tales from the Crypt* have long been obsessions of mine and I love the format of short-form horror. So this is kind of a send up to those old pulp rags.

Have you dealt with the same theme(s) in other works that you have written?

The hip-hop idiom and culture is something that exists pretty abundantly in a lot of my work. Just music in general is always present in some form in my work. It's one of the Aristotelian elements. I take that seriously. And, like I said, I've been a horror nerd for a long time now.

What writers have had the most profound effect on your style?

Stephen King, Jane Jacobs, James Baldwin, Amiri Baraka, early Mamet, Alan Moore, Grant Morrison, Sam Keith.

What were the biggest challenges involved in the writing of this play? For example, was there a particular moment that was difficult to write, and if so, why?
The hardest assignment to give to a writer is to say: "Write anything"!

Pure terror. Anyway, just deciding what to write about was the hardest thing. Once I knew what it was, it was all fun.

What is your playwriting "origin story"?
It all happened by accident. I was bitten by a radioactive dramaturg and now here I am.

How did you research the subject? Are any characters modeled after real life or historical figures?
No comment but, ya know...Easter eggs.

What is your writing process?
Coffee, morning, music playing in the background.

Shakespeare gave advice to the players in *Hamlet*; if you could give advice to your cast, what would it be?
Have fun with it. It's not that deep. It's called a "play" after all. Feel free to make big choices. There's nothing precious here.

When you're not writing, what might we find you doing?
You may see me traipse across your TV screen from time to time. I act as well as write. Or obsessively hunting down rare vinyl. Or making beats. I'm a music nerd. Or, or, or, I don't know...a lot of things.

About the Author

Ramiz Monsef is a Los Angeles-based actor and writer. Regionally he has appeared at Berkeley Rep ***(Eurydice, Arabian Nights, Fêtes de la Nuit)***, ACT (***The Time of Your Life, The Unfortunates***), Yale Rep ***(Eurydice)***, Seattle Rep, Actors Theatre of Louisville ***(Chad Deity, Glory of the World)***, The Mark Taper Forum ***(Archduke)***, The Kirk Douglas ***(Vicuna)***, The Geffen Playhouse ***(Guards at the Taj, Mysterious Circumstances)***, and seven seasons at The Oregon Shakespeare Festival where he premiered the musical he co-wrote, ***The Unfortunates***. New York credits include SecondStage ***(Eurydice)***, The Culture Project ***(Betrayed)*** and New York Theatre Workshop ***(All the I Will Ever Be)***. On TV you may have seen Ramiz on *NCIS, Training Day, SWAT, SEAL Team, Kidding, Shameless, Modern Family, Young Sheldon* and Comedy Central's *The Watchlist*. He also is in the film *SYNCHRONIC*. As a writer, Ramiz is a member of the 2019 Geffen Writers Room and is currently workshopping his newest show ***The Ants*** at the Ojai Playwrights Conference.

DREAM

by Velina Hasu Houston

CAST OF CHARACTERS

HELENA, female, biracial Japanese and Black American, 16.

LUCA, white-appearing Latinx male who identifies as white American, 16.

DUCK, female who identifies as white American, 16.

SETTING

2020, Junction City, Kansas. A high school gymnasium.

(Lights up on an empty gymnasium. Studying the vastness of the gym, HELENA enters pushing a cart full of decoration items. Outside, wind whips and the gym sighs. Helena takes this in.)

HELENA: I know, I know! Another school dance, people tracking all over your floors in tight shoes and way-too-high heels, stuff taped to your walls, and a DJ playing songs folks like me never heard of. And in five days? How am I going to get you decorated for prom in five days! Especially when everybody who used to be on the committee'll probably quit because I'm in charge now.

(The gym sighs again.)

Yes, prom's the same thing year after year. I know. That's why the ritual of that annual dance doesn't mean anything to me.

(Off, a door is heard closing and the indecipherable voices of a group of students walking by are heard. Helena looks in the direction of the sounds.)

Most kids'll think I'm crazy for talking to you, but somehow I think you're part of the universe, like the moon and stars and everything else, just like Mom's stories tell me. I'll tell you one thing: if I'd known being senior class president meant I was in charge of prom decoration, I'd've hidden out in Japanese Club instead. At least there, people understand the universe stuff.

(As she unpacks the cart, LUCA enters.)

(Truly surprised:) You're staying on the committee?

LUCA: Someone's got to make sure the prom decorations are okay.

HELENA: I was sure once I announced my interpretation of the Shakespeare theme, you'd quit.

LUCA: It's a stupid way to think about Shakespeare.

HELENA: But it is a way to think about him. It's in what he wrote.

LUCA: Tell me the truth: Do you really want to be senior class president, or did you do it so Duck wouldn't win? 'Cause you don't seem to be that interested in decorating for prom.

HELENA: We just felt it was time for a change.

LUCA: Who's "we"?

HELENA: Students like me. With foreign parents. With different kinds of looks.

LUCA: Different from what?

HELENA: From people like you.

LUCA: I thought you didn't like it when people say stuff like "those people."

HELENA: I didn't say "those people."

LUCA: Well, I'm not "people like you," okay?

HELENA: Fair enough. I guess I meant people like Du—I mean Kimberly's parents—sorry, I know she's your friend, but...they contested the election! It was as if they wanted to leave me with as few days as possible to decorate for prom.

LUCA: What're you talking about? They're not like that.

HELENA: Oh, really? Well, prom's in five days, so maybe they are like that.

(The gym sighs and Helena reacts, but Luca doesn't notice.)

LUCA: And here we are, getting this old gym ready for the biggest night in our lives and the person who should be decorating it isn't.

HELENA: I think it's sad prom is the biggest night of your life.

LUCA: It's just a dance, but it's special to a lot of people. Like Duck. She's been planning it in her head for years.

HELENA: Luca, there've been nearly 100 proms in this gym. I'd say it's tired of the same old stuff.

LUCA: Gyms aren't tired or happy or whatever. They're just gyms.

HELENA: So, I guess you think I'm crazy like Kimberly says, huh? Ruining prom because of my twilight dream theme?

LUCA: Well, it is *Midsummer Night's Dream*.

HELENA: Do you even really know what night looks like? Ever looked at all the colors and stars?

LUCA: Colors? It's dark, people don't want to be in it, and bad things happen. And who cares about stars? Waste of time.

HELENA: They're part of the universe.

(Luca sighs. The gym does, too. In response, Helena looks around the gym – but stops when she realizes Luca is watching her.)

LUCA: So… are there really African American characters—"twilight" characters—in Shakespeare, or are you making it up?

HELENA: Well, they're Africans, not African Americans, but Black people. Like Othello; he's a prince! And another prince, the Prince of Morocco! And, of course, the evil Aaron. What's a story without an evil Black guy, right?

LUCA: None of it's real! It's just stuff Shakespeare made up.

HELENA: He didn't make up anything! He adapted stories from history and usually from other countries.

LUCA: *(Stares at her for a moment and then:)* Who are you going to prom with?

HELENA: I suppose you're going with Kimberly.

(Lights shift to DUCK sitting on a splendid sofa, a television's glow illuminating her as she snacks and channel-surfs. Luca enters with donuts. He smashes his body next to hers and snuggles.)

DUCK: Stop!

LUCA: Don't be mad at me for staying on the committee. I need to soften some teachers. But Helena's doing it all wrong.

DUCK: I should write a letter to the principal! There's only one reason she got class president over me. No way I got the second most votes!

LUCA: But wasn't your great-grandfather Korean or something? Didn't you write about that in your college essay?

DUCK: Don't tell anybody or I'll kill you! *(A lie:)* It's not true anyway.

LUCA: It isn't?

DUCK: I don't want to talk about history, okay! Anyway, aren't you Mexican or something?

LUCA: My grandparents came from Argentina, but—

DUCK: So who are you to talk? You never say you're Mexican!

LUCA: I'm not. Anyway, my ancestors are all Italian and German. I'm white!

DUCK: I'm not having fun anymore.

LUCA: Sometimes life isn't fun. Here, have a donut. You know, if Helena got sick or something, you'd become president since you're vice president.

DUCK: Hey, you're right! She could fall off the bleachers or something when she's decorating!

LUCA: I don't mean that kind of something.

DUCK: Well, Luca, it's going to take that kind of something. I'm not saying kill her; I'm just saying she could get a little hurt, you know, hurt enough to stay home.

LUCA: Maybe I should just quit the committee.

DUCK: No, you're right. It's perfect. You stay on it, get really friendly with Helena, and act like her ideas are great. Then one day when she's trying to hang some witch-ass picture on the gym walls and you're spotting her, make something happen.

LUCA: What do you mean by "get really friendly" with her?

DUCK: Why is that the only thing you heard?

LUCA: Duck, it's weird, but the gym—I don't know—"feels" her.

DUCK: What are you talking about?

LUCA: What if she's a witch?

DUCK: Those people do <u>not</u> have special powers!

LUCA: But she looks at stuff different than we do.

DUCK: Why are you feeling sorry for her?!

LUCA: I don't know. I mean it's just a dance.

DUCK: Just a dance?! Luca! It's <u>prom</u>! You know that!

LUCA: Right. Prom.

DUCK: The biggest night of our lives! And what do we get? *Midsummer Night's Dream*? Oh no—we get "twilight dream." What is that?

LUCA: Do you know Othello was Black and he was a prince? I guess it's like us. We had a Black president.

DUCK: His mother was white.

LUCA: My parents voted for him.

DUCK: Oh, I'm so sorry. You must have been embarrassed.

LUCA: No—no, I wasn't. I guess your parents didn't vote for him and you weren't embarrassed?

DUCK: That's none of your business!

LUCA: If it's my business to make someone fall, then it's my business to know who your parents voted for. And who your great-grandfather was.

DUCK: Luca, this is about prom, not my relatives.

LUCA: Unless you think the way you do because of them.

DUCK: Whose side are you on? Do you "feel" the gym, too?!

LUCA: No, no, of course not.

DUCK: You better not!

(They make out as lights shift to the gym. It's the next day, after school. Helena unfurls a banner with beautiful, magical images of solely Black men and women interspersed in an equally magical scene. There is a ladder in the background. Luca enters.)

LUCA: Hey.

HELENA: Hello.

LUCA: Looks like things are moving along.

HELENA: One more night of decorating and we should be able to finish. I got the theatre students to help. They're going to make a kind of twilight with lights, stars and fairy figures.

LUCA: Nice of them to help.

HELENA: Teamwork.

LUCA: Yeah. Sorry I'm late. Your banner turned out nice. I see what you mean about twilight dreams.

HELENA: We just have to hang it where people can really see it. Maybe right there.

LUCA: But don't you think more people will see it if it's down here at eye level?

HELENA: No, I think higher is better.

LUCA: But I'm afraid of heights.

HELENA: I'm not. I'll climb the ladder.

LUCA: Uh, did you do something to your hair? You look more Asian-y.

HELENA: "Asian-y"? I flat-ironed it.

LUCA: Oh. Looks good.

HELENA: As opposed to it being more curly if I don't flat-iron it? That looks bad?

LUCA: Never mind! Damn [Gee], I'm just trying to say something nice!

(A pause.)

HELENA: Prom, the biggest night of your life! Puts you in a good mood, huh?

LUCA: *(A pause:)* You know—it's kind of—I don't know, brave doing Shakespeare this way.

HELENA: Really? I think it'll make everybody in school hate me.

LUCA: Maybe for a minute, but who cares?

(The gym sighs more intensely, and Helena looks towards the sound.)

Oh, you care. Well, don't.

HELENA: But I only have a couple of friends as it is.

LUCA: You got me.

HELENA: We're friends?

LUCA: Well, sure. I guess we kinda are now. Kinda seems like it.

(Duck enters the gym in a cheerleading uniform.)

DUCK: Hey there!

LUCA: Duck!

HELENA: Hello, Kimberly.

DUCK: What an interesting banner!

HELENA: I'm just about to hang it.

LUCA: You know, I really can handle it. Let me—

DUCK: Guys always think we women can't do anything. You climb that ladder yourself, Helena, and show him what's what. I'll spot you. Luca, go blow up some of those lovely green and brown and black balloons.

LUCA: But—

HELENA: *(To Luca:)* It's okay. Didn't you say you're afraid of heights?

DUCK: Luca, I know at prom you want to say you hung the banner for us helpless girls, but—

HELENA: *(To Kimberly:)* I thought you quit the decoration committee.

DUCK: Right, well, I walked by and saw what a great job you were doing and I realized I was just jealous. Go ahead and climb the ladder. I got you, girl.

LUCA: *(Not wanting to go through with Duck's plan:)* But—

DUCK: <u>I got her</u>.

(Helena smiles and climbs the ladder with the banner. Duck holds on to the base of the ladder. [For safety, please be creative with staging regarding the ladder, climbing and "falling."] With every

step Helena takes, Luca's anxiety increases. For Duck, the fact that her plan is unfolding makes her uncomfortable; she doesn't want to be an unpleasant, mean person. A sense of remorse crescendos in her.)

HELENA: Wow. I feel like I'm way up in the air like stars!

DUCK: *(Her remorse growing, a comment on her unexpected feelings:)* Yeah, you never feel like you think you will...

LUCA: Be careful, Helena!

DUCK: *(Remorse intensifying:)* Yeah, be careful.

(Duck tries to grip the ladder more tightly, but as she does so, she inadvertently causes it to wobble. Helena slips and falls. As Duck screams, Luca runs up and catches Helena. The trauma of it grips Duck, but Luca and Helena experience chemistry in the fall and catch. They gaze at each other in a new kind of way.)

Oh no! Are you guys okay? Oh goodness, this is all my fault!

(Luca looks at Duck thinking she did it on purpose. Duck takes this in and then:)

It was an accident!

HELENA: It was just a few rungs. I think I hurt my pride more than any—

DUCK: *(With genuine guilt:)* I'm so sorry! I was trying to hold on more tightly, then my hand slipped and—oh forget it! I'll call a teacher!

(Duck runs out to get someone.)

LUCA: You okay, Helena?

HELENA: Of course. You okay?

LUCA: Yup.

(Duck runs back in.)

DUCK: Guys, I can't find anybody!

HELENA: I'm fine.

DUCK: You sure?

HELENA: Yes.

DUCK: I'll stay and help you decorate.

HELENA: Really, Kimberly?

DUCK: Of course! And you can call me Duck.

LUCA: That's real nice of you, Duck.

HELENA: Thanks!

(The gym sighs again, but this time it's a sound of relief and release. Helena looks around.)

LUCA: What are you looking at?

HELENA: The gym.

DUCK: Uh, duh, it's a gym. Did you hit your head?

LUCA: *(Maybe he does, but he's not admitting it:)* I don't hear anything.

DUCK: *(As she strains to hear:)* I don't either. 'Cause there's nothing to hear.

HELENA: In the stories my mother read to me, the universe was alive. All of it.

(Blackout. End of play.)

The Author Speaks

What inspired you to write this play?

I was inspired to write this play based upon cultural collisions and misunderstandings that occurred when I was decorating for my high school prom. Whenever I've visited high schools in my literary travels, students have shared similar types of experiences with me. As the years go by and attitudes towards diverse cultures evolve, these kinds of tensions evolve—or, as in the case of this play, ***Dream***, they are cloaked in other types of tensions that lead to the same type of conflicts.

Was the structure or some other element of the play influenced by any other work?

The structure was not influenced by any other work. The substance of the play is influenced by my own cultural background. Being immigrant-kindred and multicultural, often our views were different from the average American students who were dedicated to creating perfect proms.

Have you dealt with the same theme(s) in other works that you have written?

I often deal with cultural dissonance in my work. By "cultural dissonance," I mean spaces in which two or more different cultures collide and/or coalesce. In such situations, it is my hope that different cultures can deepen and broaden their perspectives of humanity via their multicultural experiences. The word "culture" also must be considered in a wide-ranging manner. For example, there is a culture of women, a culture of men, a LGBTQI culture (within which there are many cultures), a Japanese culture, etc. In fact, there is not a single culture—in my view—that is monolithic. Within every culture, myriad dimensions exist out of which massively distinct perspectives can emerge. Beyond cultural dissonance, my work explores the fluidity of borders. As people interact and get to know one another, shifting across borders becomes less challenging than first believed. In this way, borders are fluid, whether they are determined by governmental edict or presumptions of the mind. My characters may be aware of them, but do not live their lives in accordance with their strictures. Even if they may in the beginning of a story I write, part of their evolution is to understand that boundaries are constructions (and usually ones that they did not build).

What were the biggest challenges involved in the writing of this play? For example, was there a particular moment that was difficult to write, and if so, why?

The biggest challenge in writing this play is the moment in which the three characters are together in the gymnasium and the possibility of a crisis looms large—the moment when Helena is on the ladder and Luca catches her when Duck inadvertently makes her lose her balance. That moment was harder to write because I didn't want the moment to reflect an on-the-nose good-guy-versus-bad-guy moment. I think such interactions are so complicated and nuanced, so I revised the moment a few times to achieve that balance.

What is your playwriting "origin story"?

I was eleven when I wrote my first play. As the multiethnic daughter of a Japanese immigrant, I faced many challenges such as being dark-skinned in a society predicated on Whiteness, being a female, being of mixed heritage, being Japanese culturally in every way possible but being in a mixed ethnic and dark body, wanting to be a writer, and wanting to be the first in my family to attend college. A military wife who taught for a year in my elementary school was an important key to unlocking the doors that so many had closed before me. She encouraged me to write a play, and I finished it. Two years later, my sixth-grade teacher had a reading of the play.

How did you research the subject? Are any characters modeled after real life or historical figures?

The play grew out of my own memories and conversations over the years with students who faced their own culminating dances. The characters are not modeled after any real life or historical figures.

What is your writing process?

I write all the time. I can write anywhere. I do not require any special conditions or environments. However, I am not a fan of loud noises. Because I don't like loud noises (like people in my vicinity playing loud music or screaming at each other), I tend to write in my backyard or in my home, which usually is a peaceful place. In a public setting, I do have the ability to sink into a story and cancel out any noise around me.

Shakespeare gave advice to the players in *Hamlet;* if you could give advice to your cast, what would it be?

If I could give advice to performers in my play ***Dream,*** I would ask them to be authentic, and consider the depth and breadth of a character.

When you're not writing, what might we find you doing?

When I am not writing, one might find me gazing at greenery in my backyard, baking, playing with my dogs or reading.

What are the challenges of writing about racial and ethnic tensions on stage?

Often, racial and ethnic tensions are veiled under other kinds of tensions. The racial and ethnic tensions are buried so that they are so systemic as to be unrecognizable, except perhaps by people of color. Writers should not be afraid to explore race and ethnicity, but must do so with authenticity and integrity. Given the times in which we live, beating around the bush should be avoided.

About the Author

Internationally produced playwright **Velina Hasu Houston** is the recipient of 28 commissions. Her work has been produced at Manhattan Theatre Club, Old Globe Theatre, Pittsburgh Public Theatre, Theatre X (Tokyo) and numerous other theatres globally. In addition to YouthPLAYS, publishers include Dramatists Play Service, Smith and Kraus, Vintage Books/Random House, *Los Angeles Times, American Theatre, The Dramatist* and others. She has written for Columbia Pictures, PBS, and several indies; co-produced *Desert Dreamers* (Peter Fonda, narrator) with Frank Suffert, and written Tamara Ruppart's critically acclaimed *Path of Dreams*. Honors include the Kennedy Center, Rockefeller Foundation, Japan Foundation, Doris Duke Charitable Foundation, American Film Institute, Pinter Review Prize, London International Filmmakers' Festival and others. At the USC School of Dramatic Arts, she is Distinguished Professor and Director of MFA Dramatic Writing. She served on the Department of State's Japan-US Friendship Commission and conducted her Fulbright Scholar specialist project at Aoyama Gakuin Daigaku, Tokyo. www.velinahasuhouston.com.

re'open our eyes

by Matthew Paul Olmos

CAST OF CHARACTERS

RAYNA

SOFIA

LUCIA

VALENTINO

CALEB

SEBASTIAN

The remainder of the classroom can be filled out as needed.

Please cast all lead roles with as many actors of color/LGBTQ as possible.

Characters may be played as any gender. Feel free to update names and pronouns accordingly.

SETTING

the present. a room in any high school.

PRODUCTION NOTES

for the "dialogue" within the stage directions, feel free to assign them to the named characters or to the student ensemble, as needed. improvisations encouraged.

(lights on a classroom which looks like every classroom you've ever seen:
rows of chairs/desks facing forward
a teacher's desk and chalkboard/whiteboard;
with perhaps handwritten history lesson topics.

history class posters posted along the walls.
a wall of windows.

however, on this particular morning,
the light from the windows is overly bright,
perhaps a hue of green coming from somewhere.

soon, various STUDENTS begin to enter;
they seem overly sleepy;
no one notices the bright from the windows.

one by one,
the students put their heads down sleepily.

until, all the students are asleep.
several moments.

then,
RAYNA shoots up as though waking from an intense dream.)

RAYNA: Whoa, whoa, whoa, what just happened?

(several students wake; look around foggily.)

Yo, did all of us just like fall asleep at the same time???

LUCIA: Shh, Rayna, some of us are *still* asleep.

RAYNA: We *did* tho', look:

(they look to the room full of sleeping or barely waking students. Rayna begins messing with her mobile.)

SOFIA: Alright, was there some party went all night an I wasn't even invited???

LUCIA: Uh, Sophie, you make it sound like you *ever* get invited.

SOFIA: You watch—one uh these days I'm gonna throw the partiest of all parties an we'll see who *I* invite.

(Rayna walks to the window; still looking down at their mobile.)

RAYNA: Yo, is anybody else's service like…not in service?

(more students wake, check their phones.)

VALENTINO: Mine must not be, cuz mine always be blowin'up.

CALEB: No bars, no Wi-Fi; networks must be recalibrating.

(SOFIA shakes their phone.)

SOFIA: Yea, yea, yer right, Rayna, mine's not doin'nothing. Lucia, yers working?

(LUCIA stands, tries to scare the room.)

LUCIA: Well, hold on. How do we know we're actually here? Maybe this is a dream an you're all in it,
or…maybe one of you is dreaming and we're all in it. Or maybe it's a nightmare.

SEBASTIAN: Or, perhaps we're all having the same dream and we're *all* in it.

(all look to SEBASTIAN.)

RAYNA: How could we be havin'the same dream, Sebastian? That don't even make sense.
This isn't one of yer poems or whatever.

SEBASTIAN: You must be right. We all just showed up, fell asleep in unison, and none of our phones work.
That makes *so much* sense.

SOFIA: Um, well, can whoever has service please call the front office an let them know the sub is late *again*.

CALEB: Sofie, what does recalibrating mean to you?

SOFIA: *Yer not a scientist, Caleb,* so stop using words you don't even know.
But wait—seriously—no one, like *nobody's* phone is working???

VALENTINO: Good morning, Sofia, nice of you to wake up.

LUCIA: Okay, okay, enough playing.

SEBASTIAN: Thank you.

LUCIA: Someone needs to—

SEBASTIAN & LUCIA: *Walk* to the front office.

(Lucia and Sebastian share an awkward moment.)

RAYNA: They right.
Who wants to come with me?

VALENTINO: Who else.

(Valentino references their own awesomeness. Sofia snorts.)

What?

LUCIA: Wherever Rayna goes, so goes Valentino.

(Valentino waves Lucia off and joins Rayna at the door. Rayna pulls on the knob, nothing; tries again, nothing.)

RAYNA: Uh, y'all, we are locked in.

(doubtful responses from students.)

VALENTINO: What's a matter, Ray, you forget how to—

(Valentino tries the knob, nothing; tries harder, nothing. laughter from students.)

Yo, shut up. Es actually stuck.

(Valentino begins banging on the door.)

Hello, we're locked in here! Somebody wanna let us out??? HELLO!!!??

RAYNA: Why do certain individuals think the louder they say something the more likely it'll happen???

VALENTINO: Same reason certain individuals think the more they talk the more interesting they'll be?

(Rayna smiles with a "let me show you how it's done" walk to the windows.
students hoot an holler in a "Awh she TOLD you!" way.
however, just as Rayna gets to the window; she stops;
all swagger gone. Rayna stares.)

CALEB: Do you need to be reminded how window sash locks operate, Rayna?

(laughter from students; Caleb assumes they're laughing at Rayna, but...are they?)

SOFIA: You so stupid, Cay—she hasn't even tried them sash locks yet.

(more laughter; Caleb now embarrasses.
Lucia notices how Rayna is staring; walks to Rayna.
Rayna points Lucia to the window; they're both staring.

Sebastian goes to them; joins in staring.
students begin to laugh nervously; uncomfortable.)

Y'know, this not even a very good joke.
I mean how funny is staring out a window?

VALENTINO: Seriously, you three look like when people see me for the first time. Can't take yer eyes off.

RAYNA: Are you two...seein'what I'm seein'?

(Sebastian nods.)

SEBASTIAN: I believe that we are.

LUCIA: But why don't you tell us what you're lookin'at. And then, we'll like...

SEBASTIAN: confirm.

RAYNA: Well, what I'm *not* lookin'at is our busted'up parking lot. Es like it ain't even there no more.

(nervous laughter from students as they look out the window; murmurs amongst them like "what's going on?" "what happened to the parking lot?"

Valentino walks in a "I'll settle this" bravado towards the window,
then stops; stares.

all are looking out the window, except Sofia, who stays looking to Rayna for comfort;
and Caleb, who stays dubiously.)

Instead, there's like…earth. Soil or whatever.

LUCIA: And grass; the greenest grass I think I ever laid eyes on.

SEBASTIAN: It's beautiful.

(students mumble in confusion.)

CALEB: Beautiful as in aesthetically pleasing the mind or the senses?

(Sophia glares at Caleb; rolls their eyes.)

RAYNA: So, instead of that chain link fence barely standing…now there's these like…vines?

SOFIA: What you mean vines?

LUCIA: From plants—there's flowered plants growing all along, with vines stretching in every direction.

CALEB: Sebastian, is that what you see?

SEBASTIAN: …it's like a growing green jungle or—

RAYNA: An when I look up at the sky…

(all look upwards.)

es like...

SEBASTIAN: the bluest blue my mind ever imagined.

(a few "oohs" and "ahhs."
Sofia and Caleb can't take it anymore,
they go to look.)

SOFIA: Omigah, I though you all was playin'some trick like yer always playin'tricks, an everyone was goin'laugh soon as I looked out, but...OMIGAH WHAT IS ALL THAT???

VALENTINO: A garden is what is that is.

(all react: "A garden?!" "What you mean a garden???"
"Lookit that, they built a garden!")

SOFIA: Did they tho'? Did they really build a garden for just us?

CALEB: Well, it is proportionately in front of us.

SOFIA: But how come? Why is it...in front of us?

LUCIA: They couldn't have built all that since yesterday.
Sofie, you an me was here till almost 5 o'clock last night—we didn't see no construction.

SEBASTIAN: What's we're looking at, would've taken days to build, maybe even weeks.

(Rayna goes to the window sash lock and attempts to open; nothing.
Valentino rushes over to help; still nothing.
as they mess with the lock, Rayna notices something outside.)

RAYNA: Whoa, whoa, whoa, lookit there!

(Rayna points at something off to the side.)

The hell is that???

(several students rush their faces to the window, trying to get a glimpse.

"What is that thing?" "Where'd it come from???")

LUCIA: ...that...is...a...brand new building.

SEBASTIAN: Okay, something is going on here. A garden is one thing, but building a building like that...would take years. It'd haffta have permits from the city, the school board had to have passed it, there would've been town halls about approving the spending.

RAYNA: But there it is anyways.

SOFIA: Es so pretty.

VALENTINO: Lookit that thing. How many stories is that???

CALEB: Does anyone else notice...how that building appears...more vivid than everything around it?
It looks...recently cleaned or—

SEBASTIAN: Like it has never been touched by human hand. *(pause.)* But...

SOFIA: But what???

LUCIA: *Why* is it there? Why is any of this there?

SEBASTIAN: Exactly.

VALENTINO: An how come we can't get to any of it then?

CALEB: It could be we're just meant to acknowledge it from afar.

VALENTINO: What, like teasing? Showing us something ain't even for us???

SOFIA: Oh, but what if we could tho'? Wouldn't that be amaze?
If outside these windows is what we saw every day.
If this is what we was surrounded with while we tried to learn all the things.

LUCIA: That'd be something, Sofia.

RAYNA: If our school looked like that, think I might even show up more often.

VALENTINO: I'd be here all early, stay extra late.

SOFIA: We could have all our classes outside even!

SEBASTIAN: Some schools *do* do that.

LUCIA: Oh yea, there are schools out there; districts all over the country, where kids get to go to schools so cleanly kept, buildings not falling apart, and green grass almost everywhere they step.

SOFIA: Where you seen a school like that, Luce?

LUCIA: Have your parents ever taken you driving, not even having any place to go, just driving wherever the car drove...an all the sudden the houses start getting bigger, with lawns all manicured or whatever?

(several acknowledgments from students:
"Yea, we drove to where there's mansions!"
"I seen a house big as The White House!")

Where those people live, their kids go to schools like that.
With all the fanciest equipment an classrooms all extra roomy.
I always thought, they prolly get up an excited every morning cuz why wouldn't they?
Who wouldn't be all tail'wagging to attend school where ya feel lucky ta even be there?

(agreements from students: "Yea, I wanna go to a school like that." "I'd never be late." "I'd get there early.")

RAYNA: Dayum, Lucia, now you got me all longing or whatever.

VALENTINO: Maybe we should just bust the windows open.

(enthusiasm from students: "Can we?" "Let's get out there!"
"Somebody break the locks!" "Break the windows!")

CALEB: And proliferate glass everywhere? No thank you. Not to mention how much trouble we'd—

SEBASTIAN: C'mon everyone, we can't just—

LUCIA: I'm sorry. I shouldn've—

RAYNA: They right. We can't be breaking anything. Chill.

(Rayna motions everyone to calm down.)

LUCIA: I shouldn't have gotten carried away.
I was just saying that places like out there do exist.

VALENTINO: Yea, but not here.

SOFIA: Why not here?

RAYNA: Cuz we don't live in them houses Luce was talking about.
Look where we live. Most of us in apartments still sharin'a bedroom.
Nothing out front but dried up weeds an dusted dirt.

LUCIA: I didn't mean to get everyone so...

CALEB: So, it *is* just for acknowledging then.

VALENTINO: Es just some dream. Some daytime'type dream.

SOFIA: So, what—we're all still asleep then?

VALENTINO: Yea, maybe so. An maybe if we all fall asleep again, things'll be back to normal.

(students react: "We don't want normal." "I don't wanna sleep.")

SOFIA: Yea, I don't know if I could sleep after this.

RAYNA: I am pretty wide open awake.

SEBASTIAN: Okay, not sleep. But just close our eyes for a—
C'mon, we could all use a few moments of just quiet...
a little time to think...?

(some students begin closing their eyes.)

RAYNA: But we *all* gotta do it tho.

(all close their eyes.)

VALENTINO: An keep'em closed.

SOFIA: For how long?

SEBASTIAN: Just a few moments.

CALEB: Uh, question: Is there anything we should be *doing* though? While we close our eyes. I do good with directives.

LUCIA: Okay, so, I know we don't live in houses like what I was talkin'about.
An maybe I should've been sad, or whatever, driving back home after seeing what some people's lives are like, but I wasn't. I *liked* being able to see what was possible, even if I prolly got no chance of ever living in a neighborhood like that, just knowing es possible is a lot.

SOFIA: Luce, you just made me real, real sad for some reason.

RAYNA: Yea, like what're we supposed to do with that?

CALEB: I'm unilaterally lost.

SEBASTIAN: Okay, wait. You said just knowing it's possible is... So, what if we close our eyes—

LUCIA: An we recreate what we saw. Picture it in our mind, any details we can remember.
This way we'll always have it with us, even if it's not there no more when we reopen.
The soil an grass all new, the plants and vines running across, the sky how wide,
an that building how inspiring.

(students all begin to recreate with their minds.)

RAYNA: Oh, I got it, I got mine *so* clear.

SOFIA: Me too. I think.

CALEB: I appreciate the guidance, thank you.

VALENTINO: I got that view mesmerized.

(several students call out: "I have it!" "I'm looking at it clear!")

SEBASTIAN: Okay, then on the count of three…

LUCIA: We're gonna reopen our eyes, an no matter what's outside the windows, we've all seen what we seen…

SEBASTIAN: Is everyone ready?

(all respond "yes.")

LUCIA: One, two, THREE.

(lights out.)

(end of play.)

The Author Speaks

What inspired you to write this play?

I've a friend who is getting her PhD on the education system in México; specifically, in how those living in small towns can gain access to university educations while still being able to live and work within their own communities. So often, people in search of a more substantial education have to leave their community to do so and often don't return. My friend's studies got me fascinated with education in the United States, in particular the topic of segregation in schools, school bussing and underprivileged districts. This play is part of my exploration of those topics.

Was the structure or some other element of the play influenced by any other work?

The element of looking out the window was inspired by an early scene in a play of mine called ***three girls never learnt the way home***, in which a busload of lower-income students is being bussed into a more affluent school district as part of a school bussing program. While the bus is en route, the students begin to notice how the landscape changes the further they get from home. In the play, the students get on the topic of rain, and why does it seem to rain more and get more green where it is more rich? I've always wanted to play with that idea more—of the landscape changing specifically because an area was more affluent—so this play takes that idea and puts it at the forefront.

Have you dealt with the same theme(s) in other works that you have written?

My play ***three girls never learnt the way home*** was meant to be the first of a play cycle dealing with the education system in the United States. However, just after writing an initial draft of that play, the 2016 election happened, and I got sidetracked into focusing on more specifically political work and the play got put on the backburner. But it is my intention to complete the cycle of plays, which would also delve into public housing and city zoning, as they have a direct impact on the topic of inequality in the United Stated education system. Perhaps this short play will lead to a larger work within that cycle.

What writers have had the most profound effect on your style?

When I started out writing I quickly discovered that I had a way with poetic language, so my early plays were very lyrical and sparse; mostly highlighting the use of poetry onstage. However, during graduate school, I was given an exercise where I couldn't use my usual language, which had in some ways become a crutch. So, writing out of my comfort zone, I wrote a piece about a lower-class family. Their language was still poetic, but it was a mixture of less educated characters talking with a rhythmic poetry. So, upon discovering my voice, playwrights like Marcus Gardley and Octavio Solis have been playwrights with influence on me. At the same time, I am inspired by the bold choices and structures of Young Jean Lee, Belarus Free Theatre, Aleshea Harris and Martyna Majok.

What were the biggest challenges involved in the writing of this play? For example, was there a particular moment that was difficult to write, and if so, why?

As I mostly write full-length plays, I don't have a lot of experience writing shorter works. So, getting in story, character specificity, and thematic discussion was all exceedingly difficult for me. For me, what the play is discussing or exploring is much more important than the plot, so I had to challenge myself to move the events along, while still getting to talk about what I wanted to talk about: inequality in education. The moment that I had to keep revisiting was towards the end when the students realize they can't have the beauty outside their window but can close their eyes and memorize it. I wish I had more pages to fully explore that, but the challenge was to get it in a way that was satisfying for a short play.

What is your playwriting "origin story"?

I never saw a play until I was a senior in college; in my family, art wasn't something that was valued in any real way. We would watch movies and listen to oldies, but that's about as far as I was exposed to any art. Still, in junior high, I began to pay attention to lyrics, and I would replace the lyrics of the songs I loved with my own. That led to short stories, and in undergrad, I had taken all the short story or creative writing courses they offered, and all that was left in general education was an Introduction to Playwriting course. So, I took it on a lark, and a few weeks in, the instructor pulled me aside and asked what my deal was, who I was as I wasn't a theatre major. She let me know that I had a talent for playwriting and should consider it. So, my senior year, I changed majors to theatre with an emphasis in Playwriting. And I saw my first theatre as a student at UC Santa Barbara.

What is your writing process?

I generally start with a topic or specific injustice which fascinates me, and then I dive into research; everything from books and documentaries to potentially visiting somewhere firsthand or speaking to people directly. And then, at a certain point, a specific detail or event will catch my eye; something that lends itself to some sort of story or character. Then I continue researching with that detail or event in mind; and soon the piece begins to unfold as I'm delving further into research. And when I have a basic idea for a play, I remove myself from the research, I set it down and begin writing. I try to write as much as I can without referring to the research so that the play becomes its own thing.

Shakespeare gave advice to the players in *Hamlet*; if you could give advice to your cast, what would it be?
Play the wonder of what's happening. Be amazed by what's outside the window.
Don't think too much about how it's happening; just let it take over and let you feel.
Why it's happening is more important than how.

When you're not writing, what might we find you doing?
I am a native Californian, so being in the ocean surfing, scuba diving, body boarding, swimming. I also love hiking with my dogs and biking. Finding interesting places to eat in whatever city I'm in is also a must.

How much excitement can be created about something the audience never sees?
My mentor Rogelio Martinez said something to me I'll never forget:
That we the theatre artists create half of the play onstage, and the other half is created in the air above the audience's heads; in their imagination. I never wish to explain everything to the audience, I want them to be participants in the theatrical experience and figure a lot of it on their own.

About the Author

Matthew Paul Olmos is a three-time Sundance Institute Fellowship/Residency recipient, Actors' Theatre of Louisville Humana Festival Commissioned Playwright, New Dramatists Resident Playwright, Center Theatre Group LA Workshop Playwright, Geffen Writers Room Playwright, Oregon Shakespeare Festival Black Swan Lab Playwright, Humanitas Play LA Workshop Playwright, Princess Grace Awardee in Playwriting, Arizona Theatre Company National Latinx Playwriting Awardee, Repertorio Español Miranda Family

Nuestra Voces Playwriting 1st Place Awardee, Cherry Lane Mentor Project playwright (chosen by Taylor Mac), and La MaMa e.t.c.'s Ellen Stewart Emerging Playwright Awardee as selected by Sam Shepard. Mentored by Ruth Maleczech through Mabou Mines/SUITE, former New York Theatre Workshop Fellow, Baryshnikov Arts Center Resident Artist, Dramatists Guild Fellow, Primary Stages' Dorothy Strelsin New American Writer, INTAR H.P.R.L Playwright, Echo Theater Company Resident Playwright and an Ensemble Studio Theater lifetime member; proud Kilroys nominator. His work is presented nationally and internationally, taught in university and, in addition to YouthPLAYS, published by Samuel French and NoPassport Press. www.matthewpaulolmos.com

THE RANDOMNESS OF BEES

by Lina Patel

CAST OF CHARACTERS

RYDER, she/her/hers, mixed-race.

CHARLOTTE, she/her/hers, any color/ethnicity.

The actors play characters who age from 9 to 15.

NOTE

Please update the *Minecraft* reference with a current popular game as needed.

DEDICATION

For Frances.

Not flesh of my flesh
Nor bone of my bone
But nevertheless, still my own
Never forget for a single minute
You weren't born under my heart
But in it.

— Anonymous

SCENE 1

(Swim practice. Starting whistle. CHARLOTTE [9] watches another group practice. She's in swim gear, backpack. RYDER [9], in swim gear and backpack, rushes on.)

RYDER: Ahhh!

CHARLOTTE: Uh—

RYDER: Bee! Bee!

(Runs, ducking and swatting.)

CHARLOTTE: It won't sting you if you stay still—

RYDER: ARRGGGHHH!!!!

(Runs offstage. A moment.)

CHARLOTTE: It's uh. It's gone. Helloo? It's gone? No bee.

RYDER: *(Cautiously re-entering:)* Are you sure?

CHARLOTTE: *(Looking offstage:)* Is that your mom? She's walking over here because you're freaking out—

RYDER: That's not my mom.

(Waves her not-mom away.)

CHARLOTTE: *(Pointing:)* Uh, well, that's *my* mom. Who your—person—is sitting by.

RYDER: I'm scared of bees.

CHARLOTTE: Noted. *(Then:)* I'm Charlotte.

RYDER: Hi. I'm Ryder.

(Whistle.)

CHARLOTTE: *(Looks toward pool:)* They're the Junior Beginners. They have another fifteen minutes. If you're here for Junior Intermediate, you're early. I'm always early to swim practice.

RYDER: I like to be early, too.

(They smile. Whistle.)

CHARLOTTE: That's Coach Bryan? When he's in a bad mood, we do backstroke.

RYDER: Ugh. I can't swim backstroke straight.

CHARLOTTE: Which swim team were you on before?

RYDER: It was—we just moved here. *(Then:)* Ch-ch-ch-changes.

CHARLOTTE: Uh, random.

RYDER: Bowie.

CHARLOTTE: My mom makes me do swim.

RYDER: Same. I'm not competitive.

CHARLOTTE: Same! My mom says I need to move more. I play too much *Minecraft*.

RYDER: I love *Minecraft*!

CHARLOTTE: Oh my gosh. Are you going to go to Woodland Elementary?

RYDER: Yeah.

CHARLOTTE: That's where I go!

RYDER: No way. I'm going to be in fourth grade.

CHARLOTTE: No way! Me, too.

RYDER: Oh my gosh.

CHARLOTTE: Can you believe school starts in a week? Summer's over?! I've been at Woodland since kindergarten. You'll love it. They don't believe in grades—or homework.

RYDER: <u>What.</u>

CHARLOTTE: And fourth, fifth and sixth grades are mixed—same room and same teacher all three years. As fourth graders, we get a sixth-grade buddy. Do you know what room you're in?

RYDER: Yeah, my mom heard a lot of good things about Room 4? So I—

CHARLOTTE: Oh my gosh! Miss Buchanan! That's my room!

RYDER: Oh my gosh!

(They smile. Ryder stops smiling.)

RYDER: Um. I'm sorry...

CHARLOTTE: Uh, for what?

RYDER: I don't know why I said that...my mom wasn't my mom.

CHARLOTTE: Oh. So that *is* your mom?

RYDER: I mean, I *do* know why—so, at the park last week this nosy lady thought Mom, who was on her cell, was my nanny. And then this friend of my mom's good friend, the *one* person we know here, was like, "I sorta see the Indian in you?" And Mom was like, "Oh, hahaha, Ryder's not South Asian!" And he was all— *(Eyes wide, mimicking a mortified adult:)* "uuhh-ohh-sorry," but he didn't have to be all: "uuhh-ohh-sorry."

(Charlotte is clueless. Ryder explains:)

I'm. Um. I'm adopted.

CHARLOTTE: Oh my gosh, I wish I was adopted!

RYDER: *(Laughs, relieved:)* What? Why?

CHARLOTTE: I have three sisters—one, I share a room with and she <u>never leaves me alone</u>. Tonee is 12 and starting at El Roble next week—the junior high—and she's like suddenly into body sprays that make me— *(Mimes gagging, then looks offstage, toward her mother:)* And that's the baby—who your mom is now holding—yes, adorable, but her farts?

(Gags again.)

RYDER: She *is* super cute. She looks just like your mom.

CHARLOTTE: Yeah, they both have big heads. Siblings?

(Ryder shakes her head, "no.")

Bliss! Do you know your—biological mom? Or dad?

RYDER: I've seen pictures. My birth mom writes us letters. Mom writes her back.

(Beat.)

CHARLOTTE: Maybe your mom can adopt me. Take me away from the madness!!

RYDER: Maybe you can spend the night! We have a den where I keep my favorite stuffies—Bubbles, a sloth, and Gramps, a cat. We can make a pillow fort and sleep in sleeping bags.

CHARLOTTE: Oh my gosh. I'll bring Slothy the First and Slothy Junior. I love sloths.

RYDER: Oh my gosh.

(They smile. Whistle. Lights.)

SCENE 2

(Three years later. Starting whistle. Swim practice. Ryder and Charlotte, now 12, enter, suited.)

CHARLOTTE: Your mom gets all weepy EVERY TIME SHE PLAYS IT—

RYDER: She's so weird. But it *is* a kinda sad song—

CHARLOTTE & RYDER: Bowie is the best.

(Whistle. Ryder stretches out. Charlotte stares toward the pool.)

RYDER: One week 'til El Roble. Six periods. Six teachers. I don't want to leave Woodland. Or Miss Buchanan. At least we can bike over together.

CHARLOTTE: Carpool. We'll get all sweaty before school if we bike.

(Whistle.)

RYDER: Oh my gosh, Charlie.

CHARLOTTE: What?

RYDER: Is it because of—*boys*?

CHARLOTTE: NO.

RYDER: Remember fourth and fifth grades? We'd all hang out—girls and boys? This year Izzy got boobs and Hannah's like six feet tall and ALL the boys got super ANNOYING. Jax and Preston do not shut up! *(Beat.)* I know you have a total crush on Preston.

CHARLOTTE: WHAT? TAKE IT BACK. WHY WOULD YOU SAY THAT.

RYDER: Smoochidy-smoochidy!

(Whistle. They help each other with sunblock. Beat.)

CHARLOTTE: Ryder? Do you think Coach Bryan is hot?

RYDER: Seriously?!

(Charlie is.)

Oh. Okay. Um... I don't know? Sometimes I think I'm asexual. I'm fluid, but sometimes I think I'm demiromantic.

CHARLOTTE: What.

RYDER: Demiromantics are attracted to people only when they're emotionally connected to them. *(Pause.)* I am NOT saying I'm attracted to you. *(Pause.)* I was for a minute at the beginning of this year, but it passed. *(Pause.)* Mom's been bugging me to write to Marianne again—happens every year at this time. August 25th is when my adoption was finalized, so Mom is always like—write Marianne! She'd love to hear from *you* instead of me and Dad! I'm always like, oh, yeah. Marianne.

CHARLOTTE: ... Uh, you're so intense.

RYDER: What does that mean?

CHARLOTTE: Like, you think about a lot of stuff all the time—

RYDER: So?!

CHARLOTTE: I'm just saying!

RYDER: Forget it.

CHARLOTTE: I didn't know August 25th was your "gotcha day."

RYDER: ... How do you know what a "gotcha day" is?

CHARLOTTE: My bestie is adopted. I read about it.

RYDER: ... Some people prefer Finalization Day.

CHARLOTTE: Noted.

RYDER: Thanks. For reading about adoption.

(They smile. Whistle. Lights.)

SCENE 3

(Three years later. Sound of birds. Ryder and Charlotte are 15. From their backpacks they put on shorts, shirts. Spread a blanket on the grass. A park.)

RYDER: I wish you guys hadn't moved. I miss you.

CHARLOTTE: I miss you, too. We're supposed to be in high school together. It totally sucks.

RYDER: You're not *that* far. With traffic an hour, but usually less.

CHARLOTTE: Yeah. I guess...I don't think I want to keep coming down. *(Pause.)* I grew up in this park. Our house is right *there*.

RYDER: I can come up more often?

(Pause.)

CHARLOTTE: I don't know, Ry. I might need...a break. Every time we see each other, I get depressed after.

(A moment. Charlotte pulls out gummy bears. Shares.)

So... How's school?

RYDER: Fine.

CHARLOTTE: How's Modern World History?

RYDER: Doing a deep dive into indigenous nations.

CHARLOTTE: Did you tell them you're part Hispanic and Native American?

(Ryder shrug-nods.)

Ry. Are you mad? About what I said about a break?

RYDER: No, no—it's our first year of high school and I just—

CHARLOTTE: At least you know people. I had to totally start over—

RYDER: Izzy went to the Catholic school, Hannah has all these basketball friends. It's huge—lots of new kids. I just don't want to explain stuff, over and over—

CHARLOTTE: Oh, like adoption stuff? Don't! Let them think whatever.

RYDER: I don't want to *lie*, but I don't want to always explain.

CHARLOTTE: Hey. Have you thought any more about meeting Marianne?

RYDER: What? Why? Is there a law that says I have to?

CHARLOTTE: Uh, no, but—we were going to meet her before I moved—

RYDER: Yeah, and then you left. Why are you bugging me about this?

CHARLOTTE: Okay, wow—you clearly feel *something* about it, so—

RYDER: Only because Mom made me see that counselor for awhile. I was depressed, but it was because you were leaving! I don't have a "primal wound"—I swear that counselor had some issues.

CHARLOTTE: Okay but, would it be so bad to meet? She's stayed in touch—

RYDER: Off and on.

CHARLOTTE: Maybe you don't want to think you're anything like her.

RYDER: No! I mean—yeah. Wait. What?

CHARLOTTE: Aren't you a little curious to see what the woman who gave birth to you is like?

RYDER: Here's a thought: you go meet her and report back!

CHARLOTTE: Ry. Just. Seeing someone who looks like you. Who you might have things in common with—

RYDER: Because she gave birth to me.

CHARLOTTE: You know you always say people make a big deal of biology, but you're making a *bigger* deal of it by pretending it doesn't matter *at all*—

RYDER: BEE.

(This time Ryder stays still. They watch the bee. The bee flies away.)

Killer bees happened because etymologists tried to breed bees that would produce more honey.

CHARLOTTE: Okay...

RYDER: They shipped African bees to Brazil, and swarms got loose and mated with European honeybees. And now we have killer bees.

CHARLOTTE & RYDER: So random.

CHARLOTTE: Maybe Marianne also has an irrational fear of bees.

RYDER: I keep thinking: what if Marianne had chosen different parents? It's so random. You look like your mom. You *sound* like Tonee. You guys are so *not* random—

CHARLOTTE: Or maybe it's all *totally* random—a random egg and a random sperm randomly meet and—

RYDER: What if she's annoying and tries to give me advice? Or wants to be friends?

CHARLOTTE: What if you love her? You may not—you may *hate* her. *That* would be awkward—

RYDER: I just wish Mom had given birth to me—it would be simpler.

CHARLOTTE: Yeah, she could have, and then the pregnancy could have caused her back issues and chronic pain and then your dad could have an affair and now they'd be divorced. Like Izzy's parents.

RYDER: Mom keeps insisting I meet her. It's like she thinks I'm missing something. I'm missing my best friend is all I'm missing—sorry—I'm glad you moved—I mean—not *glad.* *(Beat.)* Maybe I should meet her, make Mom happy.

CHARLOTTE: Your folks just want you to know everything you *want* to know—if you want to know it. They just want to help—

RYDER: But I don't need help. I'm not broken!

CHARLOTTE: We're all a little broken, maybe? Ish?

RYDER: I don't know what that means also why do you have to be so deep.

CHARLOTTE: I'm not deep. You're complicated.

RYDER: I am not complicated! You're manic.

CHARLOTTE: I am not manic. You're bipolar!

RYDER: You're so lame for moving away!

CHARLOTTE: And you're a total loser for rubbing it in!

RYDER: I'm sorry! *(Pause.)* Really. *(Pause.)* Maybe I should meet her.

CHARLOTTE: It's like—yesterday we were having pillow fights, and now Tonee is dating this skater dude who shaved his head.

RYDER: Oh, boy.

CHARLOTTE: Ry, you don't have to do anything with Marianne if you don't want to. I don't mean to confuse you. I'm sorry.

RYDER: Charlie? I understand if you need to take a break. Let me finish. I had never lied about my mom before that day—the day we met? We'd just moved, I was nine and I lied. Which felt wrong. So, I told you the truth. You didn't even care—

CHARLOTTE: What if I had? And I was like, "EW, YOU'RE ADOPTED?!"

RYDER: *(Laughs, grows serious:)* My point is. I get it. I understand if you need...space.

CHARLOTTE: ... You kinda made my point for me, you know.

RYDER: What point?

CHARLOTTE: You took a chance. And we became best friends.

RYDER: I guess we did, didn't we?

(They smile. Lights.)

(End of play.)

The Author Speaks

What inspired you to write this play?

I wrote this play to imagine and capture my daughter's experience as a young adoptee. I have had so many conversations with adoptive and biological families, adoptees and adoption counselors since becoming an adoptive parent over a decade ago. I wanted to offer a different, affirming and contemporary take around the feelings of adoptees. Adoption has become more mainstream; however, there is still contention and confusion in the open-adoption community around presumed adoption-related trauma. Adoption-related trauma was not acknowledged in the past. We've come a long way, but some believe there is an over-correction going on. In domestic open adoptions today, trauma is assumed, whether there is evidence of it or not. While adoption-related trauma may indeed be true for many adoptees, it is not the experience of all adoptees. As with most things, it is usually the more dramatic news that makes news, so I wanted to present an authentic experience of an adoptee as I know it. Also, transracial adoptions provide plenty of opportunity for misunderstandings, and that is something else the play tries to capture in a humorous way.

Have you dealt with the same theme(s) in other works that you have written?

I have dealt with the theme of chosen or adoptive families in three other works. The first was a commission from Silk Road Rising in Chicago exploring ancestry and identity through DNA testing. They commissioned ten playwrights, including the wonderful David Henry Hwang and Phillip Gotanda, and had us take DNA tests. What each of us wrote was inspired by our results. I had recently become a parent, and I was interested in exploring the theme of nature vs. nurture. In that play, the adoptee, grown into an adult and working as a scientist, imagines her birth parents' and her parents' first meeting. The second work grew out of a commission from Chalk Repertory Theatre in Los Angeles. Chalk Rep is a site-specific theatre company, and our location was the Page Science Museum near the La Brea Tar Pits. For my play, it was the location where the (pregnant) birth parents meet the adoptive parents they have chosen for the first time. It was a comedic exploration of the tough but loving decision birth parents make and the desires and careful considerations of hopeful adoptive parents. Mostly it was about how family is made: through the love of many people who want what's best for the unborn child. The third work was developed in a nine-month writer's workshop at Center Theatre Group in L.A. It became a full-length called ***The Ragged Claws***. It's set fifty years in the future, in a world scarred by climate change, and it's about what happens when the adopted son of a power couple questions his mother's politics. In a lovely, full-circle way, David Henry Hwang, who I first met in Chicago for the DNA Trail commission, nominated it for Cherry Lane's Mentor Project.

What writers have had the most profound effect on your style?

I have read everything David Henry Hwang has written and am always blown away by his structure and the incisiveness of his works. As an actor, the first writer's group I felt I truly belonged to was Jose Rivera's, which started in his living room in Hollywood. I'd studied and performed in Jose's plays as a college student, so after I got used to the idea that he was now a friend, I reread his works and talked his ears off. In group, I was privy to his birthing and crafting of new works. Finally, Paula Vogel absolutely floored me during a two-week boot-camp for commissioned writers at Yale. Each of these writers encouraged me to take risks, follow my gut, and imagine who was sitting in the audience and how I wanted to make them feel.

What is your playwriting "origin story"?

I moved from India to Los Angeles when I was young and got very sick on the way over. By the time I was diagnosed with a neurological condition, I had had a few surgeries. Complications from those surgeries meant that I missed a lot of school. I was lonely and my parents both worked, so I turned to books. I started writing short stories, plays and probably some very bad poetry from the time I was eight years old. In high school, I found my people in the drama department. I discovered Ntozake Shange, Maria Irene Fornes, Chekhov, Shaw, Jose Rivera. Thanks to a terrific drama teacher, Patty Edwards, I competed and won first place in a dramatic interpretation competition. I got a scholarship to go to NYU. After that, a fellowship to USD/The Globe Theatres. Acting fine-tuned my ear for dialogue. Being in writers' groups as an actor helped me understand structure. It was Jose Rivera's writer's group I wrote my first play in, at his urging. That play made it to Pier Carlo Talenti's desk at the Taper, and he invited me to CTG's year-long writers' group. The play I developed there got me a commission from Yale, and after that, I increasingly focused my attention on writing for theatre. At New Harmony Project, I met Meredith Steihm, who put into my head that I lived in Los Angeles and ought to try writing for television. She and her husband, another terrific writer, helped me craft my first pilot. I applied to the Warner Brother's Writer's Workshop. That's when my TV writing career began. Writers have always been the reason I've moved forward. I try to do the same for actors who want to write or younger writers—read their work, offer notes, make recommendations and share what I know to help them get what they want.

What is your writing process?

It depends on what I am writing. For a full-length play, I will often write the scenes I most want to see, out of order. Then, I might stop and write out character bios. Then I'll go back and keep writing until the play seems to have reached an end. At that point, I let myself read pages. I make myself read all the way through, without stopping to edit and tinker. After that, I will go back and begin the real process of writing, which is rewriting. Everything is up for grabs. I will cut things I love. Once I have what I consider to be a first draft, I will reach out to a writer for specific feedback. I am very mindful to reach out only when I am ready for serious notes. It's hard to read a play. It takes time and effort. I value my reader's time. Once I get notes, I'll work on a second draft. Then, I gather actors to read that draft and continue to make adjustments.

Shakespeare gave advice to the players in *Hamlet*; if you could give advice to your cast, what would it be?
Don't reach for the characters you're playing. You are enough.

When you're not writing, what might we find you doing?
I am a working parent. If I am not writing, I am helping my daughter with homework, reading a draft of my scholar-husband's book or article or madly cleaning the house—which serves the dual benefit of calming me and helping me think through sticky plot points of whatever project I am working on. I love to take long walks, listen to music and podcasts, and gather in small groups with friends to talk about writing. I need a social life, but in small doses. I love being alone when I can be.

Has being a parent made you a better writer?
Being a parent has made me less precious about what I write. Being a parent means that a lot of my friends are the parents of my daughter's friends—people not in my field who I would not have met otherwise. They are also potential audiences for my work. I love having a diverse group of friends and a community that is not an echo chamber of my own beliefs, likes and dislikes. I don't want to write only for people who love theatre, but for people who have yet to discover it or think they'll be

bored by it. When I write, I think of who my audience is, and while I always like to imagine all my favorite playwrights, actors and mentors in that audience, I also think about the friends I've made through my daughter: the plumber, the audiologist, the Mormon homemaker, etc. It's thanks to my daughter and her excellent taste in little people that I've met friends, as an adult, who have expanded my world in ways I could not have predicted. Being a parent has also made me a more empathetic audience member.

About the Author

Lina Patel is a writer/performer whose work explores power, family structures and the struggle for purpose in a precarious world. Lina was awarded an NEA grant for her play ***The Half-Breed Spy, or How I Learned to Love Imperialists.*** Her near-future play, ***The Ragged Claws,*** was nominated for Cherry Lane Theater's Mentor Project. Selected commissions/residencies: Yale Rep, Playwrights' Arena, Center Theatre Group, Silk Road Rising, Japanese American National Museum, Chalk Rep, Sewanee Writer's Conference (Walter E. Dakin Fellow) and New Harmony Project. Lina also writes for television, most recently, Ava DuVernay's anthology series, *Cherish the Day*; previously, DC's Superman origin story, *Krypton*. More at linapatelwriter.com.

A NEW STORY FROM RABBIT AND FROG

by Randy Reinholz

CAST OF CHARACTERS

ALEX, organized and always gets an A. They care about presenting the correct answer. No particular race.

LOU, a fun trickster with the attitude of "...we don't have to get it right. It's an old story, no one will know if we are making it up." BIPOC.

RIVER, a withdrawn poet who also knows culture. BIPOC (Indigenous, Latinx or Black).

The gender pronouns should be changed to best reflect the identity of the performers in the production.

SETTING

An unnamed border town along the US and Mexico demarcation. The present.

ACKNOWLEDGMENTS

A New Story from Rabbit and Frog is based on the Kumeyaay story "Rabbit and Frog" as narrated by Jon Meza Cuero, recorded by Margaret Field, translated by Jon Meza Cuero, Amy Miller and Margaret Field, included in *Inside Dazzling Mountains: Southwest Native Verbal Arts*, edited by David L. Kozak.

(An unnamed border town along the US and Mexico demarcation. Day. A room next to the school auditorium.)

(ALEX, and LOU debate the upcoming performance. Lou presents strange movements and physicalizations of the character, Frog.)

LOU: Something like this?

ALEX: Not like that. It's a Kumeyaay story, not a frog disco.

LOU: Well, something's not right with him.

ALEX: Why is Frog a him?

LOU: Frog is lazy, cocky and pushy. That's a guy.

ALEX: Maybe that's the guys you know, but the old story doesn't specify the gender.

LOU: The story says "he" and "him."

ALEX: Those are filler pronouns. Nothing in the story specifies their gender.

LOU: It doesn't matter as long as we fill the story with energy. *(Beat.)* Check it...

(Lou moves as a dancing Frog on "the make" toward Alex playing Rabbit.)

What's up, girl?

ALEX: No, no, no. I will play Frog.

LOU: No problem. *(With swagger:)* I can rabbit with the best of them.

(Lou begins to hop around.)

ALEX: *(As Frog:)* Dude. *(To Lou:)* Dude is unisex! *(As Frog:)* Dude, let me in.

LOU: *(As Rabbit, hopping:)* Not by the hair of my chinny, chin, chin.

ALEX: That's the wrong old story.

LOU: Rabbit has a hairy chin.

(Lou continues hopping.)

ALEX: Our story isn't about a pig building a stronger house. It's about Indigenous people letting strangers into their homes, like Rabbit lets Frog into their home.

(Lou stops.)

LOU: I thought it was funny. Frog talks his—*their* way into Rabbit's house, then eats everything.

ALEX: The story isn't funny, because Rabbit represents Native people and Frog represents invaders.

LOU: I keep thinking that at the end of the story, when Rabbit leaves, they're going to get other rabbits to push Frog out of the house.

ALEX: But the old story just ends with Rabbit leaving to find a new home, like Native Americans were forced off their lands.

LOU: Because they were put on reservations.

ALEX: I think River's grandma tells it as a warning, so that it doesn't happen again. Either way, we need to rehearse for this presentation.

LOU: How could River not be here for the all-school showcase selections?

ALEX: I'm going to ask Ms. Biggs not to partner me with her again.

LOU: So you get to say "her"?

ALEX: That's how *she* identifies.

LOU: I identify that she's a slacker.

ALEX: That's the pot calling the kettle black.

LOU: How's that not racist?

ALEX: It's an old expression: pot and kettle, like you calling River a slacker.

LOU: I work hard.

ALEX: You make it up as you go along.

LOU: Improvisation, baby. I'm here—showing up is halfway to winning.

ALEX: The important half is learning the material.

LOU: Well, if River doesn't show, I could probably make up a song for the beginning.

ALEX: It's not your song to make up. The old stories matter.

LOU: You've been here less than a year, but you're an expert on old stories? All we need is River to sing the Bird Song.

ALEX: Let's start from the beginning of the lines, after the Bird Song.

LOU: Then we can decide how to cover River's lines before we get called in for judging.

(Alex and Lou begin lines from the "original" story. During the first few lines, they transform into Frog and Rabbit.)

(As Rabbit:) It's an old story.

ALEX: *(As Frog:)* It's old.

LOU: It's old,

ALEX: It's old, I say,

LOU: *(As herself:)* How many times do we say, "it's old"?

ALEX: *(As herself:)* Five in all—there's one more.

LOU: *(As Rabbit:)* It's an old story, but—

ALEX: *(As mysterious Frog:)* Long ago,

LOU: *(As the mysterious Rabbit:)* people,

ALEX: people were here,

LOU: they were in this place.

ALEX: They were not people,

LOU: they were animals.

(Lou and Alex begin their respective animal movements.)

ALEX: *(Referring to Lou's animal movements:)* That's pretty good.

LOU: Thanks – they're gonna dig my Rabbit.

(Lou's Rabbit movements becomes more exaggerated.)

ALEX: *(As mysterious Frog:)* They were animals, but

(Alex's Frog movement becomes more exaggerated.)

LOU: *(As mysterious Rabbit:)* they were like people.

(Phone alarm goes off.)

ALEX: Five minutes till they decide if we are good enough.

LOU: River's such a jerk.

(After overhearing, RIVER enters. Brief silence.)

RIVER: Hi.

ALEX: Hi.

LOU: Hi.

RIVER: You rehearsing?

LOU: We are.

ALEX: For the selection committee.

RIVER: Sorry. Go ahead – I'll catch up.

ALEX: We were at *(As mysterious Frog:)* "They were animals, but – "

(As themself:) Lou, your line's next.
(As mysterious Frog:) They were animals, but—

LOU: *(As mysterious Rabbit:)* they were like people.

ALEX: *(As mysterious Frog:)* They spoke the People's Language,

LOU: they came, and they went,

ALEX: they went all over the world,

(Silence.)

River, that's you.

RIVER: What?

ALEX: I say, "They went all over the world," And you say, "They spoke the One People's Language."

RIVER: Right. *(As a character in the story:)* They spoke the One People's Language,

LOU: *(As mysterious Rabbit:)* they came, and they went,

ALEX: *(As mysterious Frog:)* they went all over the world,

(Brief pause.)

(To River:) And...?

LOU: *(Saying River's line:)* And, they spoke the One People's Language.

RIVER: I... I...

LOU: Come on.

RIVER: It's too hard today.

ALEX: Why?

RIVER: My sister was missing all night. This morning we found out that it was just because she hooked up with her stupid boyfriend. My Mom was freaked out, because *(Beat.)* Simon...

LOU: Right.

ALEX: Right, what?

RIVER: It's just...

LOU: *(To Alex:)* Her cousin, Simon...suicided.

(Beat.)

ALEX: I'm so sorry. It must have been before I moved here.

LOU: Simon was a good guy.

RIVER: Tomorrow is the second anniversary. He would have graduated this May.

ALEX: I wish I had known.

LOU: There's just stuff we don't want to talk about.

ALEX: I'll tell Ms. Biggs we need to postpone.

LOU: The other judges are in there.

RIVER: And—Grandma's here.

ALEX: Why?

RIVER: She's the one who made me come today. Said I had made you two a promise, so we have to tell our family's story.

LOU: Wow.

RIVER: Grandma says everything'll be alright.

LOU: You don't owe us anything.

ALEX: Your grandma gave us *Rabbit and Frog* for the presentation.

RIVER: And she expects us to perform it for them.

LOU: Not often we get to tell "old Kumeyaay stories" at this school.

RIVER: Yeah. All the other teams are doing presentations about Norse gods of war.

ALEX: We need more rehearsal.

LOU: We can improvise the parts we don't know!

ALEX: We have to respect the way your grandma told it to us.

RIVER: I'm not sure. Today, Grandma's story makes me think of Simon.

ALEX: But we are doing *Rabbit and Frog*, right?

RIVER: Like Lou said, there's stuff people don't like talking about. But I miss Simon and I want to talk about him.

LOU: The day he died was awful.

RIVER: But there were so many good days. When he laughed, we all laughed. I miss the joy he brought us.

LOU: So your story is about remembering Simon, the good stuff.

RIVER: A good story.

LOU: And a good time to tell it.

ALEX: What about others who are struggling? If you say what Simon did was alright, couldn't that make others...?

LOU: What?

ALEX: Well—that folks thinking about doing what he did, might *do* what he did?

RIVER: I wouldn't want that. But, I hate not to talk about Simon. We can remember the good times, even if we also remember that—

LOU: He left us too soon—and he didn't have to.

RIVER: Simon left because the darkness took away all the light he had. Today we'll remember him with everyone, so they know that when joy leaves, it can and will return.

LOU: We honor Simon's memory, to honor those we have lost and give hope to anyone struggling.

ALEX: Wait—we told Ms. Biggs that we were telling your grandma's story. What if the judges only want an "Indian story"? They may not like you making one up.

RIVER: Our story is true, and it's still my family's story.

ALEX: They are expecting something about Native people standing up to colonization.

RIVER: Maybe that's what people want from Indians, stories about the past.

LOU: But scratch the surface on those old stories and they are filled with pain that is still here.

RIVER: Grandma went to a boarding school, just like the ones where they're finding mass unmarked graves. This week they found over 600 bodies—of children. They didn't just take our land, they murdered us.

LOU: So this is how you stand up to colonization now.

RIVER: We have to stand together, to move through our pain to make room for hope and joy. We were gonna tell folks that if other people hurt one of us, they hurt all of us. And now we're gonna tell them, if one of us hurts themselves, they hurt all of us.

ALEX: This story is about getting beyond the hurt.

RIVER: We'll encourage folks if they are down.

LOU: Today, Rabbit wins.

ALEX: Can you tell Grandma we'll perform it the way she taught it to us for the summer festival?

RIVER: I will. Now, let's tell this one.

LOU: Can I still do my "Rabbit" dance in this new presentation?

RIVER: Yeah, that will make Grandma laugh.

(Lou starts the exaggerated Rabbit hop.)

(The door opens, and we hear an offstage voice say, "Next." The three friends move toward the door.)

RIVER: A good time for Simon's story.

ALEX: I get to know him.

LOU: And we can all show them the dance.

(They all dance off as lights fade.)

(End of play.)

Additional Resources

National Suicide Prevention Lifeline. Available 24 hours. Languages: English, Spanish. 1-800-273-8255 (TALK).

American Foundation for Suicide Prevention
https://afsp.org/suicide-prevention-resources

Additional suicide prevention resources, as well as study guide questions and writing prompts, are regularly updated at randyreinholz.com.

Synopsis of the Old Story, "Rabbit and Frog"

"Rabbit and Frog" is an old Kumeyaay (pronounced like lullaby, KOOM-e-YI) story. It is available in spoken word format and in print—and also translated into Kumeyaay and Spanish, so students watching the play can study the source material as desired.

Synopsis: Frog hops by Rabbit's house and asks to enter. Rabbit says no. This goes on for a while. Frog is persistent, Rabbit finally relents. Rabbit has to feed and care for the guest. Frog loves being attended to but contributes nothing. Frog eats everything Rabbit can bring until Frog becomes so fat that Rabbit no longer fits in the home. Rabbit is forced to leave and find a new place to live.

The Author Speaks

What inspired you to write this play?

Right before the pandemic, I traveled to a reservation with Kalani Quepo, whose musical ***Missing Piece*** is in development for Broadway. While there, we visited the high school on a Monday to research Kalani's script. We learned that the previous Friday, one of the bright shining stars of that community had taken his life. We were breathless. I remember losing far too many of my friends from youth to suicide, overdoses and other untimely deaths. Plays often use the events as plot points, but I wanted to offer a play to invite conversations that I didn't know how to have in my youth. In adulthood, I have had help processing those losses.

I always look for a way to laugh, too. Laughter is the best medicine. I wanted to write something that felt like it was light and fun—and the heavy subject could be buoyed by the resilience that I know helped me continue to champion the voices of marginalized communities. I know people need a place to laugh, to find their own path from innocence through loss to healing, hope and understanding.

Was the structure or some other element of the play influenced by any other work?

I always think the audience needs to laugh with characters before they care for them. Working with so many Native theatre artists, I have also observed a dedication to laughter in the face of adversity in their work and the ability to talk about the tough stuff in life. As Margaret and I worked together, looking for respectful ways to stage the original Kumeyaay story, it became clear that the story of staging the story was the story. Young people hold themselves accountable for changing social norms and values, even when the older generation may not hold these evolving norms as dear. ***A New Story from Rabbit and Frog*** is the hopeful story of intergenerational respect leading to new understanding.

Have you dealt with the same theme(s) in other works that you have written?

I find much of my work is intergenerational. In Native culture, elders are valued, respected and sought out for advice about important life matters. I also enjoy writing about the big life decisions made by young people. In my play ***Off The Rails***, set in the 1880s, the young characters have been removed from their communities and elders through the U.S. Boarding School System. So the "elders" visit as spirits. To some extent, the offstage character Simon is a spirit in ***A New Story from Rabbit and Frog*** who wants his story told. Both stories are about how young people look for balance between the harm caused by loss and the hope for new ways to navigate an ever-changing world.

What writers have had the most profound effect on your style?

I have worked with so many gifted playwrights at Native Voices at the Autry for many years. Some of the playwrights that have impacted me most: Diane Glancy, Marie Clements, Joy Harjo, Joseph Dandurand, Margo Kane, Drew Hayden Taylor, Greg Sarris, James Lujan, Vincent Whipple, William S. Yellow Robe Jr., Carolyn Dunn, Jaisey Bates, Alan Kilpatrick, Laura Shamas, Julie Pearson-Little Thunder, Kenneth Williams, Terry Gomez, Holly Stanton, Susie Silook, Robert Owens-Greygrass, Kimberly Norris Guerrero, Shaun Taylor-Corbett, Jason Grasl, Darrell Dennis, Vickie Ramirez, Vicki Mooney, Mary Kathryn Nagle, Larissa Fasthorse, Jennifer Bobiwash, Vera Starbard, The Native Voices Artist Ensemble, Frank Katasse, Joseph Valdez, Duane Minard, Ty Defoe, Rhiana Yazzie, Claude Jackson, DeLanna Studi, Dillon Chitto, Ed Bourgeois, Montana Cypress, LaVonne Rae Andrews, Lee

Cataluna, Jay Muskett, Camaray Davalos: Kira Eckenweiler, Kholan Studie, Beth Piatote, Bruce King, William Lang, Judy Lee Oliva, Tomson Highway, M. Scott Momaday, Kyle Puccia and Kalani Queypo.

What were the biggest challenges involved in the writing of this play?

It is always delicate to work with "old stories." There needs to be reverence in tandem with audacity. There are a range of permissions to obtain. No one from beyond the culture can represent the culture, and we always have to be on the lookout for what is private and what is public in Indigenous cultures. Thinking about the reciprocity of Native theatre, in that "one story" generates the need to tell other stories, we begin to understand the old story in a new context of present circumstances. So the old stories cause new stories to come forward.

What is your playwriting "origin story"?

I was a classically trained actor, seeking to work with other talented Native American theatre artists. That desire went unfulfilled for some time. I had written a few plays, screenplays and television episodes before 1994, but it was during my tenure at Native Voices that I learned the idea of reciprocity and how to tell the stories I value and believe can make a difference in American culture. I've written more about this journey as part of *Cultivating Leadership: A Primer for Academic Theatre Programs*, an Association of Higher Education publication, in the chapter titled, "Global Citizenry and Community Outreach or Strategies to enact community engagement practices that create good neighbors, support global understanding, and lead to intentional actions."

How did you research the subject? Are any characters modeled after real life or historical figures?

A New Story from Rabbit and Frog is based on original, sustained community engagement between Margaret Field and Kumeyaay communities in the US and Mexico. Over a period of ten years, Margaret worked with elders on language and cultural preservation. The story of "Rabbit and Frog" was originally told by Jon Meza Cuero. You can read more about Margaret's work on the SDSU website.

What is your writing process?

My writing process has a few steps. I come up with a story, create the backstory of the characters, and clarify the arena, the place the story takes place. I beat out or plan the major events of the script. In the case of ***A New Story from Rabbit and Frog,*** I discovered that telling the story was the main action. Then it was time to write a first draft. During the writing, the characters develop their own voices and need to speak. I follow those impulses and modify the beats of the script to keep the forward action of the play moving.

Once I have a draft, I work very hard to get actors to read the script to me. Sometimes we begin with me reading it to them, and then they read it back to me. Then questions follow. I sort through the questions, ask friends to read the script to provide additional notes. Then I arrange a second reading. If the questions are focused on a few areas of need, I send the script to readers who give very vigorous notes. I repeat that process until I like the script. Sometimes it is weeks, other times months. It takes as long as it takes. Structure matters.

From my foundations in theatre as an actor, writing dialogue is a pretty straightforward process. Working with actors that are appropriate for the roles provides greater insight for tone and nuance in dialogue that sounds authentic to the audience.

Shakespeare gave advice to the players in *Hamlet;* if you could give advice to your cast, what would it be?
My advice for artists working on this script is to think about the origin story of "Rabbit and Frog." Ask basic human questions. Who would tell a story like this? Why are the lead characters animals? Discuss the layers of metaphor in the old story and see how they apply to the new story. Get to know the people in the play as well as those whose lives are represented on stage during the telling. Performers in ***A New Story from Rabbit and Frog*** hold space for those who were denied the chance to speak for themselves.

On playing the show: Have fun! Be respectful as you would with your aging grandparent's stories. Laugh and find joy. Explore hope at the end of the show. Play it in a way that gives folks hope.

When you're not writing, what might we find you doing?
My life has been making theatre. I have worked professionally since my 20s and have been a university professor for over 30 years. It has been an obsession since the early 1980s. I do like gardening. The older I get, the more I like to spend time with people I know well.

One of my favorite activities is traveling to see a friend's work. I always combine work travel with time to see different things that aren't available where I live. I love historic sites that are not focused on arousing patriotism, but instead offer insight into how people lived in the past and what can be learned about how to improve my life today. I also love to spend time with my dog.

My greatest joy is spending time with my wife, Jean Bruce Scott. Jean has such an impressive career and has been so generous to share her knowledge and love with me since the late 1980s.

We don't have any Indigenous students or audience members, so is this show right for us?
Well, yes, it is for you! First, don't assume you know someone's identity. At times, people with Indigenous heritage may be reticent or don't know how to talk about it, and family stories can be complicated: Err on the side of inclusion. And regardless, it is time to tell Native stories from Native people, particularly in the United States of America. All of this land was once territory of Indigenous people. As factions of 21st-century U.S. citizens talk about their heritage, tradition and family rights, it is important to remember that many Indigenous families' lines began 10,000 or more years ago. It is time to hear and see the rest of the story. Plays written by Native authors open up those lines of history and tell the whole story of who we are and where we live. They are even more vital today than at any other time in our history.

About the Author

Randy Reinholz, an enrolled member of the Choctaw Nation of Oklahoma, co-founder and producing artistic director emeritus of Native Voices at the Autry, is an award-winning producer, director, actor, activist and playwright. Reinholz has produced more than 30 scripts and directed over 75 plays in the United States, Australia, England, Mexico and Canada. ***Off the Rails***, his bawdy and irreverent adaptation of Shakespeare's ***Measure for Measure*** had its world premiere and sold-out run at the Oregon Shakespeare Festival. A tenured professor at San Diego State University, he has served as Head of Acting, Director of the School of Theatre, Television, and Film, and Director of Community Engagement and Innovation for the College of Professional Studies and Fine Arts. Awards: Ellen Stewart Award for Career Achievement in Professional Theatre, Playwrights Arena's Lee Melville Award, LA Drama

Critics Circle Gordon Davidson Award, SDSU's Outstanding Faculty Award, Los Angeles City/County Native American Indian Commission and City of Los Angeles Award for Outstanding Contribution to the Los Angeles Community.

METALHEAD THREAD

by Elizabeth Wong

CAST OF CHARACTERS

MEWTON'S PAW, female.

FLIPPY2236, non-binary.

SALTY PICKLE, female.

GROUND CONTROL, female.

SETTING

The Internet. A music message board. Think Reddit or Quora. Not Zoom!

In real time. The present.

PLAYWRIGHT'S NOTE

To keep current, you may substitute popular artists or bands in favor in the future, but please do keep the flavor of the original intent. About costumes, maybe indicate socioeconomic backgrounds with clothing; perhaps only Ground Control wears Goth clothing and makeup.

PLAYWRIGHT'S ACKNOWLEDGMENTS

Thank you, Jonathan Dorf and YouthPLAYS: so happy to share a collection with my fellow BIPOC playwrights. This play is dedicated to my brother William Wong, who introduced me to all kinds of music whether or not I wanted to listen.

(Suggestion: Huge headphone projected onto a screen. Or maybe, a large human skull wearing earbuds. Or maybe, a big Reddit-like balloon.)

(Screeching industrial metal or noise music, as the music fades to half–)

(Spotlight up on MEWTON'S PAW, or perhaps this character simply enters. Everyone in the play wears headphones or earbuds, heads banging hard!)

(Suggestion: As Mewton's Paw speaks, sound of typing or tapping on a keyboard underscores the dialogue. This could occur whenever a character speaks, and follows the cadence of that speaker.)

(Music fades out!)

MEWTON'S PAW: When someone asks me how I'm doing, I put this on. It's pure insanity. *(To self:)* Uh, no, insanity not the right word. Backspace backspace, backspace backspace, backspace.

(Backspacing – she's rewriting what she just wrote.)

It's pure—*chaos*. Yes, that's the perfect word, *chaos*.

(Spotlight on FLIPPY2236.)

FLIPPY2236: I find the sound…

(Typing pauses, then resumes –)

…invigorating, like Rachmaninoff.

MEWTON'S PAW: Replying. Flippy2236, Rachmaninoff? He your music teacher?

FLIPPY2236: Replying. Mewton's Paw, you are just sad. I been telling you since inception, dude, broaden your musical horizon.

MEWTON'S PAW: Replying. Flippy2236. Dude, what are you, my mother? Is Rachmaninoff a sub-atomic penetration? Because if it don't go rapid fire through my skull, my ears ain't for sale.

FLIPPY2236: Replying. Mewton's Paw. That link you just sent gives me lockjaw and I can't talk until I punch someone's face.

MEWTON'S PAW: Replying. Flippy2236. Now that's what I'm talking about. Violence of sound, so inspirational.

(Spotlight up on SALTY PICKLE.)

FLIPPY223: Hey, look who's here? Salty Pickle!

MEWTON'S PAW: Hey, Salty Pickle!

SALTY PICKLE: Oh my god! Dudes, I just felt my bones sink deeper into my skin from that bass drop.

MEWTON'S PAW: I feel like I'm being chased by bears and eaten by a pack of hungry hyenas.

SALTY PICKLE: Is this track on Spotify?

MEWTON'S PAW: Yes, yes it is!

FLIPPY2236: Spotify doesn't pay artists squat diddly unless you're Drake or Ed Sheeran. It's exploitation.

MEWTON'S PAW: The system.

SALTY PICKLE: The system.

FLIPPY2236: Yeah, the system—join it, fight it or steal it.

MEWTON'S PAW: Or stomp, shred, destroy it.

FLIPPY2236: I just played your insane track for my sibling. They is way older, and said—get this—"How can your generation dance to this?" So I sez to MeiLing, "Like this:"

(Flippy2236 mimics a seizure.)

MEWTON'S PAW: Hahaha. ROFL. Flippy2236. You got skillz. So accurate. [Translation: Rolling On The Floor Laughing.]

SALTY PICKLE: So accurate. When I was ten, my uncle and me used to stay up Saturdays until six in the morning, watching Metalocalypse, Aqua Teen, anime. Out of all of that, the music pumps were my favorite, of which this style very much resembles.

FLIPPY2236: Question. Putting it out there. Is this pitch shifted? Sounds a semi-tone lower, just curious.

MEWTON'S PAW: Replying. Salty Pickle. Nah, it's the original recording. Phenomenal instrumentation as foundational. With some of the most profound lyrics out there backing it up.

SALTY PICKLE: Shit yeah, I'm feelin' it. [Expletive can be deleted.] This is gonna be my daily Reddit session soundtrack from now on.

FLIPPY2236: This makes me want to play Wii [Pronounced: Wee] Tennis without the safety strap. LOL. [Translation: Laughing Out Loud.]

MEWTON'S PAW: This track makes me want to call my dentist, tell him to say "ahhh" and power up the drill.

FLIPPY2236: It's the soundtrack to my mental illness.

SALTY PICKLE: If *madness*...hm, write something smarter...backspace, backspace.

(Backspace tapping sounds.)

...if *schizophrenia* was a sound, it would sound like this! It's not your normal darkness. It's like a mixture of industrial Beastie Boys and tribal warfare. IMHO. [Translation: In My Humble Opinion.]

MEWTON'S PAW: Agree! It's perfect for my music fight with the neighbors upstairs. They listen to rocky mountain highs, country roads and sunshine on their body parts.

(All but Flippy2236 react with disgust.)

FLIPPY2236: Yo, I like John Denver.

MEWTON'S PAW: *(Ignoring:)* Stormtroopers of Death is the reason I'm fit. I play it loud through my headphones. It makes me feel like I'mma subatomic particle traveling faster than the speed of light. Salty Pickle, comment?

SALTY PICKLE: Mewton's Paw, replying. As a marching band nerd, I appreciate the samples of marching snares and quads. It's like a theme song for the dark web.

MEWTON'S PAW: Wait. What? Flippy2236, did you just write, you like John Denver? Are you flippin' insane?

FLIPPY2236: I like John Denver. His voice is sweet. Soars pure, like an eagle. Until he crashed his airplane.

MEWTON'S PAW: Flippy2236, are you a girl? You like Ariana Grande and Justin Bieber too? Insert!

(On screen: Face With Mouth Open Vomiting emoji.)

SALTY PICKLE: LOL. Flippy2236, use the upside-down face for sarcasm. Because Mewton's Paw thinks you're serious.

(On screen: The Upside-Down Face emoji to denote sarcasm.)

FLIPPY2236: I'm *not* a girl. And what if I was?

MEWTON'S PAW: I don't need emojis to detect sarcasm. Insert!

(On screen: The Happy Devil emoji to denote annoyance.)

SALTY PICKLE: This music is too angry for girls.

FLIPPY2236: Girls get angry.

MEWTON'S PAW: This music is too complex for girls.

FLIPPY2236: Angry girls don't just pout or sulk or sigh. Maybe they slash tires. Maybe they run away from home.

SALTY PICKLE: Or they cut. Or worse.

MEWTON'S PAW: Or maybe they write long emails because they want closure. They like boy bands who like it that way. They like K-Pop.

(All react with disgust, except Salty Pickle.)

SALTY PICKLE: Dude, I think B.T.S is cool. K-Pop is cool. It's better than the Baby Shark Song Remix. Insert.

(On screen: Shark emoji.)

MEWTON'S PAW: Get off this thread, you pansy. This is hardcore, not *Sesame Street*!

FLIPPY2236: Mewton's Paw. It's a free country.

SALTY PICKLE: Mewton's Paw. What you wrote is just ignorant.

MEWTON'S PAW: Metal is for men! You girls sound like a bunch of sissies.

FLIPPY2236: Mewton's Paw, stop with the derogatory gender references. I'm nonbinary. I like heavy metal. I've made 300 posts on this message board. That's why I'm here on this thread, to discuss intelligently. And I don't appreciate being put into the constraints of a small-minded category of who listens to what music. Insert, emoji.

(On screen: Person Shrugging emoji, to indicate indifference.)

SALTY PICKLE: Well, if we're all pulling back the curtain. I'm a girl, and I like raw sound. I don't see the point of this cul-de-sac.

MEWTON'S PAW: Wow? *(Beat.)* Mind blown. I mean this is a subcategory thread dealing with the black sheep of metal, and the both of you have been on since inception. We've talked Throbbing Gristle and Cromagnon. Wow, this is the ultimate catfish.

FLIPPY2236: So I can't be on this thread anymore because I don't identify with your normatives!? You're not the moderator, Mewton's Paw!

SALTY PICKLE: You know a lot about the subject, but it's not because you are a guy.

MEWTON'S PAW: Guys, guys. I'm a girl too.

FLIPPY223: What?! **SALTY PICKLE:** What?!

MEWTON'S PAW: Yeah yeah, I'm female.

(They all bust out laughing.)

(On Screen: Astonished Face emoji.)

(Lights up on GROUND CONTROL.)

FLIPPY2236: Hey, look who's on the thread!

ALL: Ground Control!

GROUND CONTROL: Guys, guys, I'm inflating the balloon.

MEWTON'S PAW: Okay, me too.

FLIPPY2236: Inflating.

SALTY PICKLE: Doing same.

GROUND CONTROL: This might not be appropriate, but here goes. Posting a link. Ever heard of this song?

(They put their hands to their headphones or adjust their earbuds, as if straining to listen to a song.)

(Playwright's Note: It's okay if we don't hear the song. However, if rights can be secured, perhaps we hear the first bar of Paul McCartney's song, "Blackbird.")

FLIPPY2236: Maybe I'm losing my hearing, but this song is delicate. *(Strains to hear:)* Hey, I know that voice. Paul McCartney, as in The Beatles. My great-grandparents listen to this.

MEWTON'S PAW: I listen to "Blackbird" ironically every time I need to go to sleep.

SALTY PICKLE: Actually, I un-ironically like it.

GROUND CONTROL: What is the guy singing about? That's what I want to know.

MEWTON'S PAW: Kill me and play this at my funeral.

FLIPPY2236: I'm glad we live in a time where memes can be a band.

MEWTON'S PAW: That wasn't a meme, Flippy.

FLIPPY2236: You know, this was once an actual recording sold in an actual store.

SALTY PICKLE: I'm hearing this for the first time. It's—kinda sweet.

MEWTON'S PAW: Sarcasm. Good one, Salty.

GROUND CONTROL: Guys, guys—trying to understand this song. Enlighten me.

FLIPPY2236: I read a random post that McCartney wrote the song as a civil rights protest. Like some racial reckoning. Like some quiet call to persevere. For the moment to arrive.

SALTY PICKLE: If he did, I just don't get it. It's so lyrically obtuse! But then again, I flunked poetry. Does have a lightness of being, sad yet uplifting.

GROUND CONTROL: It's like when you first listened to Gorillaz. Like you question yourself—why are you listening to noise? But then you keep coming back to it again and again, and eventually you realize, you actually like it.

MEWTON PAW'S: For me, jury's still out, so no.

FLIPPY2236: This song is dope. Glad you are discovering something new, unlike some closed circuits on this thread. Thanks for the link. Guys, I gotta go, gym class. Logging off.

(Lights out on Flippy.)

MEWTON'S PAW: Well, it's my first time. It's a pretty tune. But I think ol' Paul is backtracking to make a song about blackbirds seem relevant. That's a metaphor for you.

GROUND CONTROL: I feel drawn to this song. Like moth to flame. In the dead of night, spread your wings? I feel this weird feeling. I mean, is this what Hope feels like?

MEWTON'S PAW: Beats me. IDK. [Translation: I Don't Know.] Dude, I listen to metal because there is no hope, only chaos and Megadeth. So take it to Facebook.

SALTY PICKLE: Ground Control, "Blackbird" makes me feel like a whole donut. Thanks for the laugh. You are hilarious. Logging off.

(Lights out on Salty Pickle.)

GROUND CONTROL: Me too. AP history teacher walking down my aisle. Ground Control out.

(Lights out on Ground Control.)

MEWTON'S PAW: Well, honestly, I can't tell whether I like this song or not. *(Beat.)* Guess I just prefer someone screaming in my ear while I do homework. Other than my stepdad.

(Mewton's Paw cranks up a heavy metal/industrial track, gets back to her homework. Slow fade to black.)

(End of play.)

The Author Speaks

What inspired you to write this play?

I was inspired by another one of my own plays. My latest non-TYA play is about a musician who enlists in the army and, lucky/unlucky him, his first deployment is at Guantanamo in Cuba during the use of enhanced interrogation techniques. Music, especially heavy metal and rap, played a big part in those interrogations. Detainees had to listen 24/7 to Eminem. And soldiers there were pumped into action by listening to this music—even at breakfast! Since I've been immersed in this music, I wondered about why some are drawn to it, why it speaks to them. ***Metalhead Thread*** is my quick, light-hearted look into an even more hardcorc subgenre of metal, and hopefully audiences and performers will find it to be a fun exploration of the message board world, as well as issues of gender.

Was the structure or some other element of the play influenced by any other work?

Oh, this is an easy question to answer. Social media and message boards like Reddit and Quora influenced this play. I just wanted to mess around with theatrical structure, have some fun with the emojis that are frequently and commonly used in everyday communication. I thought it would be funny if a message thread came to life, basically looking for a way to express a written two-dimensional medium in a live immediate flesh-and-blood three-dimensional way. Which is all blah blah blah. Simply put, I wanted to see if I could mimic the way random people communicate on these specialized messaging threads and if they make connections—and even influence each other—without ever having met. It's all just words on a screen. Nothing Zoom-y here, because that would ruin the fun of this play.

Have you dealt with the same theme(s) in other works that you have written?

I am interested in smashing stereotypes, so yes, I have done this in other plays, usually in relation to the misconceptions related to being an American of Asian descent. I'm also interested in amplifying women and the experiences of women and representing women in popular culture, so yes, I have usually written plays with female protagonists. I like to see reflections of myself. I want to expand the definition of girldom, womanhood...by throwing out the confinements of definitions and labelling that are so convenient for people to use. Throw it, toss it, or expand it and embrace it.

What writers have had the most profound effect on your style?

My style changes depending on the needs of the play and the characters who inhabit that play. But the writers who have the biggest effect on the social activism in my work are writers of the Harlem Renaissance. Stylistically, I'd say playwrights like Bertolt Brecht, Megan Terry, Luigi Pirandello, Frank Chin, Genny Lim, Aeschylus and Eugene Ionesco. Also, the musicality of words is a big influence, so poets like Gwendolyn Brooks, Naomi Shihab Nye, T.S. Eliot, Tristan Tzara. I like surrealism, I want my plays to soar, but be tethered loosely to reality and terra firm through humor.

What were the biggest challenges involved in the writing of this play? For example, was there a particular moment that was difficult to write, and if so, why?

The biggest challenge was letting go of a cool character in the first draft. I wanted Paul McCartney to join the message board and talk about his creative process to a bunch of nerdy narrow-minded metalheads. But after a couple days of procrastination, I just hit delete to his character. I murdered him from my play.

What is your playwriting "origin story"?
Oh, this is a good one. I quit my job as a newspaper reporter at *The Hartford Courant* on April 1 when the world was younger. I didn't know what I wanted to write, so I gave myself the gift of a year to figure it out. One day, I was in New Haven, CT, at a stationery store with a friend who was a student stage manager at Yale Rep. She knew August Wilson, and there he was standing in one of the aisles. She introduced me as a new playwright. I was immediately humiliated, as I hadn't written a single word yet. But he was so kind: He regarded me and simply said, "Of course you are. You're a playwright." OMG! We parted, and later that evening, I stayed up long into the morning writing my first play, ***Aftermath of a Chinese Banquet***. Every new playwright writes their family dysfunction play, and that was mine. It has never been produced, because I thought it would cause an explosion in my family and I didn't want that, but it did get me into graduate school. Validation and encouragement from August Wilson gave me the kick in the pants I needed to start writing, and I haven't stopped since.

How did you research the subject? Are any characters modeled after real life or historical figures?
Nah, no real research, as I've contributed to message boards like this; the ones I do involve astronomy, one of my current passions, and I've "hung out" on sites like Quora and Reddit while researching other plays.

What is your writing process?
I procrastinate as much as I can. I read, I research, I think a lot...it might last a couple of agonizing months of non-writing. I think about all those writers who can write on a daily basis and feel an overwhelming envy. Then, just when the deadline looms and I think I won't, I do. My subconscious mind works on the problem when I sleep. And I trust my subconscious and intuition as long as I feed these muses with information. And in

very quick vomitus of words, I'll have a solid first draft to work from—and I'll wonder where the heck that came from. That's generally how it works. Procrastinate. Panic. Voila, The Play.

Shakespeare gave advice to the players in *Hamlet*; if you could give advice to your cast, what would it be?
Don't signpost or signal or giveaway the twist of the play. Stay in the moment: This isn't Zoom or FaceTime, this is a message board come alive. So characters can focus on their love of music, and not on who they are. ALSO, for a director's note, I would suggest characters ignore each other until it's impossible to ignore, because that moment of "seeing" the other characters, I think, will be a source of delight. And to all designers, for the most part, work against type visually. Perhaps only Ground Control is your classic Goth in black, chains and tattoos.

When you're not writing, what might we find you doing?
You might find me at an astronomy outreach at an elementary school or a star party on the lawn or parking lot of an observatory with my gorgeous eight-inch Zhumell Dobsonian Reflector telescope. Or watching reruns of *Star Trek: The Next Generation* or *Star Trek: Deep Space Nine*. I'm also volunteering as a citizen scientist to hunt for exo-planets, which sounds exciting, but it's all about looking at a bunch of graphs filled with data. If I see a dip on the graph, it means a possible planet has caused its sun to dim in brightness. Just call me exo-planet hunter!

Why include a non-binary person in your play?
Why not!?! :-D Turns out my non-binary character is the most open-minded person in the play and is more broadly educated in music, which is my easy metaphor for being receptive and responsive for all that life has to offer. If you are in a subgenre, get out of it and embrace other genres. This has implications for being broad-minded about a lot of things, not just taste in music. I want to expand and normalize the definition of what it

means to be human. You feel me? I hope so!

About the Author

Elizabeth Wong's award-winning plays for family and young audiences include ***Tam Tran Goes to Washington*** (East West Players), ***Boid & Oskar*** (Cincinnati Playhouse in the Park), ***Prometheus, Goloshes of Fortune*** and ***Amazing Adventures of the Marvelous Monkey King*** (Denver Center Theatre), ***The Magic Bird Musical*** (Honolulu Theatre For Youth), ***The Happy Prince: The Pop Opera*** (Kennedy Center for the Performing Arts), with music by Emmy-Award winning Michael Silversher. She co-wrote with novelist Jeff Gottesfeld the stage adaptation of Randa Abdel-Fattah's *Does My Head Look Big in This* and Josh Hangarne's *The World's Strongest Librarian*. Ms. Wong is a Disney Studio Writers Fellow, a regular guest editorial columnist for *The Los Angeles Times* and a writer for Margaret Cho's ABC sitcom *All-American Girl.* She holds an MFA from NYU's Tisch School of the Arts, teaches playwriting at Boston Conservatory@Berklee and is a proud member of PEN, Writers Guild of America and the Dramatists Guild of America. Her website is www.elizabethwong.net.

sunset on seb and hiro.

by christopher oscar peña

SETTING

where the sand meets the sea. just before sunset.

WHO

seb, a person of color.

hiro, a person of color.

gender and pronouns can be adjusted for the performers.

A NOTE

a playwright smarter than me once said, "show the strings." meaning, we all know we're seeing theatre! less is more. use your imagination and think of the most creative ways to do something on stage. often times, it's the cheapest, simplest thing you can do. the theatre shouldn't feel like *avatar*. it should feel like human beings sitting around a campfire telling each other a story. trust the actors and the words. that's all you need.

DEDICATION

to Lee Killam

for giving me the ocean.

(the ocean

soft waves crashing

that moment right before sunset

SEBASTIAN enters
he wears converse and skinny jeans
a zip up hoodie
under the hoodie he's wearing a Smiths shirt
this is a guy who doesn't do the beach
he stares at the water
the waves crashing

crash
crash
crash
crash
crash
crash
crash
crash

solitude

after a moment he takes off his hoodie and we realize that his shirt is torn
Sebastian looks around
is he looking for something
or someone
he is careful not to be seen
as he takes off the torn shirt

when he takes off the shirt we see two bumps on his back
they look like broken bone protruding from his scapula

finally HIROKI enters
he has jet black hair

he wears boardshorts and a tank top
there is a silver sheen to his skin)

HIROKI: there you are

SEBASTIAN: where else would i be

HIROKI: don't know
you took off so quickly
didn't wait for me
thought maybe

(Sebastian doesn't say anything)

let's go into the water

SEBASTIAN: no

HIROKI: come on

SEBASTIAN: absolutely not

HIROKI: you promised

SEBASTIAN: i told you
i'm scared

HIROKI: don't be
i'm here
i'm here with you
i won't let anything happen

SEBASTIAN: you can't promise that

HIROKI: yes i can

SEBASTIAN: no you can't

HIROKI: Sebastian

SEBASTIAN: just stop it okay

(a moment)

HIROKI: you're not wearing a shirt

SEBASTIAN: i'm sorry
i'm pretty sure you were there
when they ripped it

HIROKI: i'm sorry about that

SEBASTIAN: save your apologies

HIROKI: i'll get you a new one

SEBASTIAN: no thanks

HIROKI: it was just a shirt
there's a million of them online
everyone has that shirt

SEBASTIAN: it's not the same
it was an original
my dad bought it at one of their concerts
they were his favorite band
he met my mom that night
gave it to me
it was special

HIROKI: i'm so sorry

SEBASTIAN: whatever

(a moment)

HIROKI: you should put your hoodie on
people will see

SEBASTIAN: I don't care
they know now
they all know
what difference does it make

HIROKI: they were all drunk
they won't remember

SEBASTIAN: i hope they do

HIROKI: i was trying to protect you

SEBASTIAN: you were trying to protect yourself

HIROKI: you don't understand

SEBASTIAN: explain it to me

HIROKI: those guys

SEBASTIAN: are trash

HIROKI: we play on a team together
you know that
we have to be cool
otherwise
it all falls apart

SEBASTIAN: that's an excuse
you want to be like them
you want to be like them because they're attractive
and normal
you want to be like them because they fit in

HIROKI: yea
so
what's wrong with that
what's wrong with wanting to fit in
be normal
have it easy

SEBASTIAN: nothing
nothing's wrong with that
you're right

HIROKI: then

SEBASTIAN: it's what i want
it's what i want
but i can't have
i'll never be like them

HIROKI: i don't want you to be

SEBASTIAN: i'll never be like you

HIROKI: don't say that

SEBASTIAN: i cut my wings off for you
i cut my wings off for you
i cut off a part of me
of who i am
i did that
for you
i changed the way i spoke for you
my language
the way i speak
spoke
i keep changing
for you
when is enough enough
it'll never be enough

HIROKI: i just wanted them to like you
i wish they could see you the way i do

SEBASTIAN: but i was beautiful before
wasn't i

HIROKI: yes

SEBASTIAN: then

(Hiroki is silent)

Hiroki

HIROKI: i don't know

(they sit in silence)

let's go for a swim

SEBASTIAN: no

HIROKI: why not

SEBASTIAN: because

HIROKI: because why

SEBASTIAN: i don't trust you

(ouch)

HIROKI: but you're my best friend

(Sebastian starts to laugh)

don't

SEBASTIAN: when they came over
he asked you
who is your best friend
me or Sebastian

HIROKI: i'm sorry
i was scared

SEBASTIAN: and you looked at me
your eyes
they were so sad
and that's when i knew

HIROKI: knew what

SEBASTIAN: you'd fail me

HIROKI: it's not a big deal

SEBASTIAN: you looked at them
at him
and you said you are
you're my best friend
and then as they ripped off my shirt
trying to see what was underneath
you just stood there

HIROKI: i didn't do anything

SEBASTIAN: you just stood there and watched
as they humiliated me

HIROKI: i'm sorry Sebastian
you're my best friend okay
do you hear me
you're my best friend
we just have to keep it a secret

(Sebastian nods his head yes)

(Hiroki is relieved)

HIROKI: i'm so glad
i'm so glad you understand

(as Hiroki takes off his shirt

we see the light of the setting sun reflecting off his body

the silver sheen reflects more and more

and we realize that the silver sheen is actually

tiny scales

tiny scales on his body

like a fish)

come on

SEBASTIAN: there are so many things that could be in the water
straws
old mcdonalds cups
spilled oil
angry piranha
stingrays with an axe to grind
needles

shattered glass
the bodies of those that have drowned
the bodies of those who have fallen off a cliff
the bodies of those who have been murdered and left for dead
ghosts
the souls of the lost
pirates
old shoes
missing jewelry
broken hearts
abandoned tires
one armed octopi
broken lipstick
all kinds of terrifying things
lurking just under the
under the
all kinds of things waiting to get you
you don't know
you don't know what waits in the water

HIROKI: come on Sebastian
you can trust me
ill protect you

SEBASTIAN: no Hiroki
you couldn't protect me on land
with them
what makes you think
you can protect me out there

(Hiroki looks at Sebastian pleading)

HIROKI: please
come with me
please
forgive me

(Hiroki walks towards the water
he extends his hand out to Sebastian
Sebastian ponders
does he follow Hiroki into the water
or does he leave

does he forgive
or does he forget

he ponders
he ponders

Hiroki pleads)

(end of play.)

The Author Speaks

What inspired you to write this play?

many things inspired me to write this play. they include a memory from my past that haunts me. a location that i initially resisted but have grown to love because of the person who took me there. and an homage to a writer that first made me fall in love with theatre when i first encountered plays. these things, and a need and desire to write parts for young actors of color, all came together to form this play. it's weird alchemy. truly, it's magic.

Was the structure or some other element of the play influenced by any other work?

when i was a kid, i thought plays were boring. i thought they were only for and about old white people fighting in large houses that had nothing to do with me or where i grew up. they also lacked magic. they felt everyday and boring. but then one day i discovered the plays of Jose Rivera. he taught me that the stage could be magical and unexpected. that the rules of regular life did not apply here. that i could make my own rules. my work isn't always so magical these days, but every once in a while, i go back to why i was first drawn to theatre in the first place. this play is a reminder of that.

Have you dealt with the same theme(s) in other works that you have written?

i think playwrights spend their lives dealing with the same themes in their work over and over and over in unexpected ways. looking at this play, i recognize some themes and questions i always revisit: what is home? what is America? who gets to be an American? can people from two different worlds ever truly connect? why are we so scared of things that are different from us? along those lines, i'm always exploring "identity." how do we define ourselves? how do others define us? are these two identities ever aligned?

What writers have had the most profound effect on your style?

naomi iizuka
luis alfaro
jose rivera
julia cho
lynn nottage
arthur kopit
brooke berman
tony kushner
david adjmi
chay yew
adam bock
melissa james gibson
jenny schwartz
caryl churchill
young jean lee
david henry hwang
maria irene fornes
eduardo machado
robert o'hara
anne garcia-romero
lloyd suh
nicky silver
wendy wasserstein
donald margulies

What is your playwriting "origin story"?

my father says that the first thing i ever told him i wanted to be was a writer. as a kid, we would go to the mall and i would definitely hide out at the bookstore for hours. i remember reading books that i was probably much too young to be reading then, and although i wouldn't say my palette was highbrow literature, it was at least diverse and representative of mass popular culture. i remember being devoted to john grisham. for a long time, i wanted to be a lawyer. i remember devouring the novels of stephen king. and i remember being obsessed with danielle steel. all while i was around the age of 13. i also read a lot of *star wars* novels, particularly the ones that followed han and leia's twin jedi children. i didn't read theatre as a young kid. if i'm being honest, i don't think i knew it existed. i didn't know where to get it, and the little theatre i'd seen, hadn't inspired me. i didn't care about the form. even then, i think i knew in the back of my mind, the form didn't care about me. i didn't truly discover theatre until college. like many, i thought i wanted to be an actor. i think most of us start that way, because it's the only really visible path we are told about or see. most of us don't really know that you can design shows or direct them. most of us don't know that you can write them because outside of new york, at least back then, we rarely saw new plays. instead, we saw the same productions of shakespeare or arthur miller. and as a young kid, those things were incredibly boring to me. i actually did not know anyone was creating new work because i never saw it. in college, i thought about dropping out of the theatre completely because i didn't actually enjoy acting classes and was going to pursue sociology so that i could go to law school later—(as an adult, i'm convinced that playwriting is actually another form of sociology and legal work tied together). i was going to drop out, but naomi iizuka, who was the head of writing where i went to college, stopped me one day and said, "you're a storyteller." every quarter for the rest of college i took a playwriting class with her or another amazing playwright that she would bring in, and then i was lucky enough to get into grad school at nyu. once i got into tisch, it never stopped.

What is your writing process?
some people write every day. i don't. i hate the revision process. it's really hard for me. so, instead, i think about plays in my head for a long time. i form images. ideas. i think about the plot and structure and where major reveals should happen. i think about all these things until about 75 percent of the play is put together in my mind. i leave some room so that i can still invent and be fresh during the writing process, but i have enough of a blueprint that i know where i'm headed. then i find some retreat or writing group—i'm very lucky to be a member of New Dramatists and to have held fellowships at places like The Lark and the Playwrights Realm whose sole focus is helping playwrights work on their plays at every stage of the process—and write the play in four or five days. by then, the play is so fully fleshed that the revision process isn't so hard.

i'm also a big fan of something that wendy wasserstein used to say: essentially, that living your life IS part of the writing process. go on walks. take in other theatre. visit with friends. spend time at a museum. go shopping. have relationships. LIVE. these things all fuel you to write plays and create stories and keep you motivated! i'm a firm believer in this idea.

Shakespeare gave advice to the players in *Hamlet;* if you could give advice to your cast, what would it be?
be honest—it's okay to be scared, sometimes that means you're doing the best work.

How was the first production different from the vision that you created in your mind?
i always leave room in my plays so that they feel and look different every time they are performed! i trust the director, designers, actors, etc. to bring their unique points of view to my world. i give them the blueprint, but they build the house. i am excited to see what color they paint the door and whether the grass is mowed or not. trust your collaborators! let them do

what they do best! that way, you'll always be a fresh audience member to your own play who still gets to be surprised by the magic they see on stage!

When you're not writing, what might we find you doing? absorbing other art and being in conversation with other artists is the best way to keep working even when you're not. i'm at the theater every night. or a movie. i go to a museum as least twice a week. i go to the ballet. be a sponge!

About the Author

christopher oscar peña is a storyteller originally from California, now residing in New York and LA. The Clarence Brown Theatre commissioned and produced the world premiere of his play ***The Strangers***. In New York, the Flea Theatre produced the world premiere of his play ***a cautionary tail***. His NEA award-winning play ***how to make an American Son*** will be produced by the Arizona Theatre Company, where he is an Artistic Associate, before moving Off-Broadway to the Rattlestick Playwrights Theatre. In television, he was a writer on the Golden Globe-nominated debut season of the CW show *Jane the Virgin* and the critically acclaimed HBO show *Insecure,* as well as the Starz show *Sweetbitter* and the Freeform series *Motherland: Fort Salem.* He is currently adapting Pedro Almodovar's ground-breaking film *Women on the Verge of a Nervous Breakdown* as a television series for Apple+.

LIKE A KNIFE

by Michelle Tyrene Johnson

CAST OF CHARACTERS

GLORIA OYA DECIMA, a black woman.

BELLA, a black teenage girl.

BEAU, a white teenage boy.

BLAZE, a teenage girl of color. She doesn't have to be black.

SETTING

In a classroom.

At a time that is no time at all and all of time.

(A classroom. Three teens, BELLA, BEAU and BLAZE, are sitting and/or standing at school desks talking intently with each other as DECIMA enters. They abruptly and obediently stop as she enters the room and stands at the head of the classroom.)

DECIMA: I hope all this talking means you have chosen.

(A beat of silence.)

Well? Has a cat gotten each of your tongues?

BLAZE: Oh no, no! In fact I was thinking of choosing cat.

DECIMA: Hmmmm. An interesting decision. Domestic or wild?

BLAZE: Domestic. I think. You mean a housecat?

(Beau tries to hide a snicker.)

DECIMA: I see, Beau, that you are amused by Blaze's choice. What have you decided upon?

BLAZE: Actually Miss Decima, I haven't decided yet. I was just thinking about picking cat. But maybe instead of a house cat, being a mountain cat would be better.

DECIMA: Oh. I see.

BLAZE: But I could go with a house cat if you think that's better. Or maybe a neighborhood cat. Maybe...

DECIMA: This isn't about pleasing me.

BEAU: See, I told her a cat was a dumb idea. They don't really have nine lives.

DECIMA: There are no dumb ideas. So what is yours?

BEAU: I'm...I'm still thinking. Maybe a breeze?

DECIMA: And you're teasing Blaze when you still are indecisive. Bella, you're being mighty quiet over there. Come to a decision yet?

BELLA: Why do we have to decide? I mean you're...well, you're in charge.

DECIMA: You are the last one I expected to hand over your agency to another. Even to me. What's wrong?

BELLA: What if we make the wrong decisions?

DECIMA: *(A beat.)* I clearly have failed you all.

BLAZE: No, Miss Decima! How can you say that?

DECIMA: Because at the moment of deciding your next great destiny you are saying things like "dumb idea" or "wrong decision." Those words or comments have never been articulated by me, yet on your decision day that is what is flooding your process.

BEAU: It's just that we've never picked for ourselves before. This is hard.

DECIMA: You are right. When you were baby beings, I decided for you because you couldn't decide for yourselves. But I know my creations. I knew, for example, that Beau would be a great blade. And you were. Right up until it was time for another being to take over the knife's existence.

BEAU: But I hurt people. Caused pain. People bled because of me. One woman even died from my cut. I know it was an accident, but—

DECIMA: That was because you existed before tetanus shots and medical solutions were discovered. You did what a knife was designed to do. All of you always did. Beau, you forget that you peeled fruit and cut food to feed a village. That was your primary purpose. *(Beat.)* So, is that why you want to be a breeze this time?

BEAU: I guess I want to be something...something that can't be turned into something else. You know?

DECIMA: Of course I know. You want to be soft. And gentle. And free. Do you know what kind of breeze, or do you want me to help you decide?

BEAU: Off of water, I guess.

DECIMA: Now you know the only rule I have.

ALL: The devil doesn't delight in details, but Gloria Oya Decima does.

DECIMA: *(To Beau:)* So what kind of breeze do you want to be?

BEAU: I was thinking one off the ocean.

DECIMA: Any particular ocean?

BEAU: I was thinking of a place where there used to be a lot of harm. I know we don't undo the past.

DECIMA: You're thinking of off the Atlantic? Where there was slave trade? Please, tell me.

BEAU: That's a dumb idea too.

DECIMA: There are no dumb ideas. Just ideas that need to be sheltered by purpose. That's all.

BEAU: Really?

DECIMA: Yes. So I think an ocean breeze off of West Africa is a fine idea.

BEAU: I've done a little research on where.

DECIMA: Of course you have. I created your very essence. And I've seen you grow. So just tell me. Where?

BEAU: I was thinking off the coast of Senegal. Near the House of Slaves. It's a museum now, you know, to let people know about the horrors of—

DECIMA: I know, Beau, I know. That's a beautiful choice. And so it is.

(Beau pauses before he exits. Blaze gives him a sign of friendly encouragement. He and Bella exchange a knowing look. Beau exits.)

(To Blaze:) At this point of your development, I only ask that you give a little thought to your choice, to have your choice sheltered by purpose. So, why a house cat?

BLAZE: My two other times I was plants. I want to be something living this time.

DECIMA: Plants are living. They grow, and if they aren't taken care of, they shrivel or they wilt. Or sometimes they die.

BLAZE: So you want me to be a plant again?

DECIMA: You are mature enough to decide for yourself. I just don't want you to underestimate your existence. Ever. Even if you choose to be a patch of grass, you matter. You are important. Your existence, no matter how seemingly small, will always mean something.

BLAZE: But so many do great things.

DECIMA: Once, a thousand years ago, when a being was too young to pick for himself, I made him an emperor. As emperor, he commanded wars that saved thousands of lives. But the first time the being got to choose for himself, you know what he picked?

BLAZE: What?

DECIMA: A blanket. A baby blanket that got handed down through the generations to help babies sleep, to soothe their fears. In fact, Jamal is still doing that. So, if you want to be a cat, you go be a glorious house cat. In fact, knock over a few plants while you're at it.

BLAZE: So it's ok? It's really ok?

DECIMA: Personally, I think you would make a better dog. But what do I know? I've only been at this a few hundred millenniums. Go. Be a cat. You've got tons of lifetimes ahead of you to be a schnauzer.

(Blaze throws her arms around Decima.)

BLAZE: Oh thank you!

DECIMA: And so it is.

(Blaze waves at Bella and exits.)

Ok. It's just us right now and clearly something is bothering you. Are you having trouble deciding?

BELLA: May I ask you a question?

DECIMA: When have you ever had to ask me if you could ask me something?

BELLA: Every time I look down, I think, this is the time when humans will get it right.

DECIMA: The devil doesn't delight in details, but Gloria Oya Decima does. So what in particular burdens you?

BELLA: All the people who judge by skin.

DECIMA: Ahhhh. That.

BELLA: They fight over skin. They judge over skin. They kill over skin. Why?

DECIMA: That is a big question. And I'm not surprised at all that it would be you asking it.

BELLA: Why me?

DECIMA: I created you to be a thinker. *(A beat.)* But I also created you with a strong emotional center to go with your brain. There's a reason, Bella, I made you human the two lifetimes you've had. You could handle it. The intensity. The complexity. The emotions.

BELLA: The contradictions. The inconsistencies. The pain.

DECIMA: The joy. The hope.

BELLA: I hated the hope. That was just a setup for the pain.

DECIMA: Even as a young being, you were always a mature soul who understood the connections.

BELLA: So why racism?

DECIMA: Do you think the creator of the human race would choose for you to hate among yourselves? I do not like seeing my creations fight.

BELLA: But you could stop it.

DECIMA: I can't stop human will. That would undo the very nature of being human.

BELLA: So you're saying people choose racism.

DECIMA: Over and over again.

BELLA: They choose all kinds of bigotries. It's awful.

DECIMA: Yes, they do. Because the nature of being human is like that of being a knife. It cuts, it kills, but it saves, it protects.

BELLA: But I want to stop racism. I want to be the one that tries. To finally be the one that makes people see how we're all connected. That the poorest person in India is connected to the richest person in America. That we really are just one race despite all the hate and all the ways we treat each other like we're separate.

DECIMA: I love how worked up you get about this. We've already had a Gandhi, a Harriet Tubman, a Mandela, an MLK. They made progress. But if you have made a choice in who you need to be, my job is to make that happen and support your journey. Even when you're not human, I still give you choice.

BELLA: You may not agree when I tell you.

DECIMA: I'm about to birth you to the first existence you have chosen for yourself. Sock it to me!

BELLA: I don't understand.

DECIMA: It's an old expression. Tell me who you want to be this time.

BELLA: I don't want to be a who, I want to be a what.

DECIMA: What is your what?

BELLA: Maybe I should be a global pandemic.

DECIMA: That is an interesting choice. What would be the purpose?

BELLA: People don't seem to listen anymore unless it's major. Epic. Unreal.

DECIMA: In the beginning, I thought about making this a blue marble of nothing but oceans and landscape. But I thought, what's the fun in that?

BELLA: But so much of being human hurts. And hurts other humans. And your other creations.

DECIMA: You say that, but you're considering a choice where many will die. And suffer. Is that what you want?

BELLA: No! No! Of course not! But can't a pandemic be like a knife that either kills or saves?

DECIMA: It's true. Good or harm can come from the same instrument. But you saw how Beau was at the thought of being responsible for the death that came from one accidental cut. And he wasn't even choosing for the knife to have that impact.

You, that's exactly what you would be choosing. Inevitable harm and death to thousands. Possibly millions.

BELLA: I guess I hadn't thought this through. It's just that humans don't seem to remember that they are all the same underneath their skin.

DECIMA: You are correct.

BELLA: But there's absolutely no guarantee that me coming back as a pandemic would stop racism. Or any other kind of bigotry.

DECIMA: You are correct again.

BELLA: Ok. Then I know what I choose.

DECIMA: I'm ready to hear it.

BELLA: I want to be a megaphone. That goes to one rally after another. If I can't stop racism, I can at least make louder and stronger the voices of the people who try.

DECIMA: As long as you realize that, like a knife, you don't get a say in who uses you and why.

BELLA: It would be easier to go back as a patch of grass. Maybe in the yard where Blaze roams or in Senegal to be with Beau.

DECIMA: You could.

BELLA: But I need to try. *(Bracing herself:)* Ok, I'm ready.

DECIMA: A megaphone it shall be. And so it is.

(End of play.)

The Author Speaks

What inspired you to write this play?

I moved from my hometown in the greater Kansas City, Missouri metropolitan area to Louisville, Kentucky in the middle of two very important events. I moved in during a global pandemic and during a racial justice protest, triggered by George Floyd but in support of Louisville native Breonna Taylor, literally outside of my window. As a black woman, as a journalist, and as a playwright, the interplay of those two major events weighed heavily on my mind as I wrote my play. I wanted to write a short, fantastical piece where there was a greater meaning for the pandemic that related to my perennial hunger for social justice. From that came ***Like A Knife***.

Have you dealt with the same theme in other works that you have written?

Several of my plays use my particular brand of Afro-futurism, where I take the inner world of black people and transform it into a more fantastic world that deals with the real issues of black people. Whether it's a young black woman accidentally thrown back to the 1940s in my full-length play ***The Green Book Wine Club Train Trip***, or whether it's ***The Green Duck Lounge*** where a black woman who doesn't age lives to witness the clarity of how the Black Lives Matter Movement is the modern-day equivalent of the Civil Rights Movement, I like the theme of black female resiliency triumphing over time and place.

What writers have had the most profound effect on your style?

I'm an odd bird. A black only girl child, with a loving family but a family that didn't quite know how the weird way my brain and imagination worked. In place of having brothers and sisters, my "peers" growing up were the television set and books. While I watched way too many inappropriate nighttime shows, my true TV love was soap operas. In fact, I tested out of kindergarten to go straight to first grade, and as my mother tells the story, what I said during the meeting with the administrator who told her this was that I was upset that I would now have to miss watching my "stories" on TV.

My favorite books were mysteries. Loved good mysteries. Powered through Nancy Drew and The Hardy Boys like nobody's business, then moved quickly on to Agatha Christie and Rex Stout, creator of the Nero Wolfe series. I loved the tight, taught, crisp and brisk style of Stout. Very character and word driven. As I write this, I realize that it is so inevitable that I would become a playwright.

As an adult black woman, I would say that the two writers who had the most profound impact on my writing were science fiction writer Octavia Butler and the gritty and iconic playwright August Wilson. Butler showed me that science fiction wasn't about green men and fantastical worlds, but worlds where the power dynamics didn't default to straight white men with a good head of hair and authoritative voices. Science fiction—at least Butler style—was about possibilities and spirituality and equality and how that moved and ruled worlds. Wilson inspired me because he wrote about the kinds of black people I knew and grew up with—raw, gritty, fast-talking, tough-spoken real folks.

What were the biggest challenges involved in the writing of this play?

You mean besides the usual back and forth of revision and suggestion and rewriting? The biggest challenge frankly was explaining the point I was trying to make about how anyone could view a pandemic in any way shape or form as having any positive benefit. My character is a young spirit, about to become reincarnated into another existence. She's over and over and over again seen how relentlessly racism mutates in all eras and societies of people—is a virus that can bring people to their knees all over the world what it takes to stamp it out? Obviously, in a longer play, I could get into that all more and better. But in a 10-minute play for younger audiences, it was tricky. But it was incredibly important to do so. Because words matter and the impressions they create and reinforce matter more.

What inspired you to become a playwright?
Words have always been my favorite way of communicating. Another big influence on my writing, my creativity, my very life really, is the late great Gordon Parks. He was a photographer, a writer, a painter, a film director, a renaissance man. And he was a black man from my home state of Kansas, only from a small town in the state. I read his book *A Choice of Weapons* in high school and it moved me to my core. In writing about his life, he talked about how he could use weapons of artillery or destruction to move through life, or he could use other tools as weapons to fight bigotry. His most well-known "weapon" was a camera—my "weapon" has been my words. Yet, I didn't become a playwright until I was 46 years old. My words were as a newspaper reporter, as a failed novelist, even as an attorney. But it wasn't until I wrote my first 10-minute play, inspired by a theatre competition that I accidentally came across on Twitter, that playwriting became my "home" as a writer. Pretty quickly everything that had ever inspired me came together in one art form. And as I wrote more plays, and more different kinds of plays, and longer plays, and more experimental plays, along with the honor of seeing them on stage, I felt like I had finally found the way to use words in a way and shape that mattered. But don't tell the newspapers, law firms or my current public radio job that I said that.

What is your writing process?

My writing process is that I have no process. I sit in front of a laptop, sometimes a notebook, and I purge. I won't use any words more gross than that. But I channel my emotions or my current problems or my current indignities into characters who feel the same way I'm feeling about something. As I've grown as a playwright, I've learned to be better at shaping my "purges" into a form and shape and craft that bring audiences in instead of putting them off because I'm being so heavy-handed. I'll admit that what I work on now—10 years later—is not going in the opposite direction of being too subtle to make a point.

Shakespeare gave advice to the players in *Hamlet*; if you could give advice to your cast what would it be?

Don't get so hung up on the realistic issues of the play that you fail to lean into the fantastical, non-realistic "conceits" of the play. In other words, let the theme of the play guide your choices, not your focus on the realistic parts.

Why is God a black woman in your play?

Black Girl Magic has bordered on becoming nothing more than a silly hashtag to throw out. But the truth of the matter is that I do think black women have a special powerful tenderness that makes the best of us the very kind of divinity most of us want and seek. Again, going back to Octavia Butler and her science fiction novels, the intersection of race and class can be almost supernatural in the right spaces. So why wouldn't I make our Supreme Being, in my play, a black woman?

About the Author

Michelle Tyrene Johnson is a public radio journalist, author and speaker from the Kansas City, Missouri area who now lives in Louisville, Kentucky. As a playwright, Johnson's plays have been staged nationally, including in California, Texas, Illinois,

Connecticut, Pennsylvania, Michigan and Kentucky. Several of her plays, such as ***Wiccans in the Hood, The Negro Whisperer, Trading Races: From Rodney King to Paula Deen, Echoes of Octavia*** and ***The Green Book Wine Club Train Trip*** have been in New York City festivals and readings. Her play ***Only One Day A Year*** was chosen for the Kennedy Center's 2020 New Vision/New Voices Festival and recently received an award from the National Endowment for the Arts for its world premiere at the Coterie Theatre in Kansas City, Missouri.

About YouthPLAYS

YouthPLAYS (www.youthplays.com) is a publisher of award-winning professional dramatists and talented new discoveries, each with an original theatrical voice, and all dedicated to expanding the vocabulary of theatre for young actors and audiences. On our website you'll find one-act and full-length plays and musicals for teen and pre-teen (and even college) actors, as well as duets and monologues for competition. Many of our authors' works have been widely produced at high schools and middle schools, youth theatres and other TYA companies, both amateur and professional, as well as at elementary schools, camps, churches and other institutions serving young audiences and/or actors worldwide. Most are intended for performance by young people, while some are intended for adult actors performing for young audiences.

YouthPLAYS was co-founded by professional playwrights Jonathan Dorf and Ed Shockley. It began merely as an additional outlet to market their own works, which included a substantial body of award-winning published and unpublished plays and musicals. Those interested in their published plays were directed to the respective publishers' websites, and unpublished plays were made available in electronic form. But when they saw the desperate need for material for young actors and audiences—coupled with their experience that numerous quality plays for young people weren't finding a home—they made the decision to represent the work of other playwrights as well. Dozens and dozens of authors are now members of the YouthPLAYS family, with scripts available both electronically and in traditional acting editions. We continue to grow as we look for exciting and challenging plays and musicals for young actors and audiences.

About ProduceaPlay.com

Let's put up a play! Great idea! But producing a play takes time, energy and knowledge. While finding the necessary time and energy is up to you, ProduceaPlay.com is a website designed to assist you with that third element: knowledge.

Created by YouthPLAYS' co-founders, Jonathan Dorf and Ed Shockley, ProduceaPlay.com serves as a resource for producers at all levels as it addresses the many facets of production. As Dorf and Shockley speak from their years of experience (as playwrights, producers, directors and more), they are joined by a group of award-winning theatre professionals and experienced teachers from the world of academic theatre, all making their expertise available for free in the hope of helping this and future generations of producers, whether it's at the school or university level, or in community or professional theatres.

The site is organized into a series of major topics, each of which has its own page that delves into the subject in detail, offering suggestions and links for further information. For example, Publicity covers everything from Publicizing Auditions to How to Use Social Media to Posters to whether it's worth hiring a publicist. Casting details Where to Find the Actors, How to Evaluate a Resume, Callbacks and even Dealing with Problem Actors. You'll find guidance on your Production Timeline, The Theater Space, Picking a Play, Budget, Contracts, Rehearsing the Play, The Program, House Management, Backstage, and many other important subjects.

The site is constantly under construction, so visit often for the latest insights on play producing, and let it help make your play production dreams a reality.

More from YouthPLAYS

Enemy|Flint by Diana Burbano
Drama. 70-80 minutes. 5-17+ females, 3-15+ males (10-20+ performers possible).

Thia Stockmann, a bright young medical student, has discovered her hometown's water supply has been poisoned. Her data, her personality and her determination offend first her family, then the town council, then the community. As her friends and allies buckle under the pressure, Thia refuses to run from doing what is right, even if that means becoming "an enemy of the people."

Xtigone by Nambi E. Kelley
Drama. 90-100 minutes. 5-15+ females, 4-15+ males (9-30+ performers possible).

Chicago. Present day. Xtigone's brothers have been killed in drive-by shootings by each other's rival gang. Her powerful uncle calls for the bodies to be buried instead of uncovering the violence in the city streets. In this re-imagining of Sophocles' ***Antigone*** that uses poetry, dance and dialogue that speak with an urban voice, will Xtigone go against his edict and risk death in her quest for her community's truth?

The Matsuyama Mirror by Velina Hasu Houston
Drama. 60-70 minutes. 4 females, 1 male, 3 any gender.

In Matsuyama, Japan in the 1600s, a world before the discovery of mirrors, young Aiko comes of age in the aftermath of her mother's death. Gifted with a "magic" mirror, she sees her image and believes that it is her mother's spirit—and when her father remarries and she begins to grow up, Aiko resists, escaping into an enchanted world where dolls come to life. As they encourage her to stay to play and frolic, will Aiko fall into the fantasy forever, or will she discover the true magic of life?

Roll of Thunder, Hear My Cry by Ed Shockley
Drama. 105-115 minutes. 4+ females, 6+ males (12-40 performers possible).

The gripping story of Cassie Logan's coming of age in Jim Crow Mississippi is brought to life on the stage. A cast of ten principal actors plus an expandable chorus performing in a stark setting transform this epic into an inspiring tale of hope and triumph in the face of adversity.

The Post Office by Melissa Leilani Larson
Drama. 50-60 minutes. 3 females, 8 any gender.

Plagued by a mysterious illness, teenage shut-in Ash longs to see the world. But she refuses to be sad, instead befriending strangers as they parade past her window, helping each one smile despite their war-torn land's darkness and dystopia. When Ash learns that the building being constructed near her home is a new post office, she dreams of a life spent delivering the mail and traveling beyond her small village in this magical and theatrical contemporary adaptation of Tagore's classic play.

Cuentos de Josefina by Gregory Ramos
Folktale with music. 100-110 minutes. 6+ females, 4+ males (10-50+ performers possible).

A heartfelt memory tale that follows the story of young Josefina and her brother Ignacio's journey from Mexico to the United States after the Mexican revolution. The play explores what it means to leave one land in search of another, and the value in maintaining ties to our past. Based on true Mexican family tales, ***Cuentos de Josefina (Josephine's Tales)*** weaves together a series of stories that can be told with various theatrical devices, including story theatre, movement, music, shadow and puppetry.

Made in the USA
Middletown, DE
09 September 2024

60045999R00113